SMART
SERVICES

SMART SERVICES

Competitive Information Strategies, Solutions and Success Stories for Service Businesses

Deborah C. Sawyer

 Information Today, Inc.
Medford, New Jersey

First printing, January 2002

Smart Services: Competitive Information Strategies,
Solutions and Success Stories for Service Businesses

Copyright © 2002 by Deborah C. Sawyer.

Library of Congress Cataloging-in-Publication Data

Sawyer, Deborah C., 1953-
   Smart services : competitive information strategies, solutions, and success stories for service businesses / Deborah C. Sawyer
       p. cm.
   Includes bibliographical references and index.
   ISBN 0-910965-56-0 (softcover)
       1. Service industries. 2. Business intelligence. 3. Strategic planning. 4. Competition. I. Title.

   HD9980.5 .S284 2001   HD9980.5
   658.4--dc21   .S284
                                2002   2001054762

Printed and bound in the United States of America.

Publisher: Thomas H. Hogan, Sr.
Editor-in-Chief: John B. Bryans
Managing Editor: Deborah R. Poulson
Copy Editor: Pat Hadley-Miller
Production Manager: M. Heide Dengler
Cover Design: Jacqueline Walter
Book Design: Lisa M. Boccadutre and Kara Mia Jalkowski
Proofreader: Susan Muaddi Darraj
Indexer: Robert Saigh

Table of Contents

PART 2
THE COMPETITIVE ISSUES

PART 3
THE COMPETITIVE GAME

First Words

In a departure from usual practice and rather than have one person write the foreword to *Smart Services: Competitive Information Strategies, Solutions and Success Stories for Service Businesses*, we invited several people to contribute and have created the following "roundtable" discussion with their comments.

Each person was given a few chapters to read, rather than the entire book—we wanted to keep the task manageable, timewise, for everyone—and so contributors shared their thoughts on those specific sections of the book they read; some people also provided feedback as to what the entire book might be like.

All roundtable participants are active in the competitive intelligence (CI) field and work with global clients. Most run their own service firms, meaning a business owner's perspective often informs their comments.

In alphabetical order, our contributors are:

Cynthia Allgaier, The Pineridge Group, Alexandria, VA, U.S.

Babette Bensoussan, The MindShifts Group, Sydney, NSW, Australia

Jane Boon, Ph.D., Northeastern University, and CI Consultant to a supply chain execution software firm, Boston, MA, U.S.

Karl Kasca, Kasca & Associates, Pasadena, CA, U.S.

Richard MacRae, Mc3 Intel, Toronto, ON, Canada

Neil Simon, Business Development Group, Southfield, MI, U.S.

Now let's give our experts the floor....

NS: First, I think the topic is great and that Deborah is tackling a topic that has not yet been covered. Chapter 1: Competitive Challenges for Service Businesses takes on the challenge of defining the nebulous service industry. This unique contribution to both the field of CI and the service industry outlines a structure that can be used by service firms to both understand their own human capital as well as to compare it to their competitors. Deborah shares her sensitivities and mental models—I'm glad that someone has taken on this challenge.

CA: It's true, as this chapter suggests, that services sector competition is messy and getting messier as relationships become differentiated while companies we compete against bundle capabilities from their extended value chain into their bids.

KK: Chapter 1, as in the rest of the book, gives a thoroughly researched review of CI. The explanation of the concept of "time" for service businesses, in this chapter, is worth the price of the book alone!

BB: Long-term planning, strategy, and CI, as we know, are not on every company's agenda, which means we are fighting against all sorts of competition, including those highlighted in Chapter 2: Customer-Origin Competition. I have personally found there are a couple of other areas where customers can compete with service firms. The classic one is where we train and educate people but have found, often after the first project, the client feels they know enough to be able to do the CI work themselves.

KK: Chapter 2 is really filled with astute insights that reflect mountains of experience, research, and reasoned analyses, but the delivery is like warm milk at bedtime—very comfortable and easy.

BB: And as Deborah has pointed out in this chapter, there is the other part to this story, where a member of a customer's staff attends a conference and feels he or she can do the work effectively. In the end, your experience and expertise count for nought in the customer's mind.

KK: Every time you see the phrase "in this case," look for gold to follow—I found myself highlighting Chapter 2 (and many other chapters) constantly; there was so much great information!

BB: One final point that hit home for me was that one of the greatest threats to any service firm is that of competing against a lack of action; a customer's inability to plan ahead or take action means a smaller market pie for everyone.

RM: Success in service sales is very difficult to cookie-cut, because of the innate human factor of the business. Although a well-prepared plan and consistent strategy are important points of departure, Chapter 3: A Matter of Influence describes why we cannot rely on a formula approach to selling services. Your relationship with influencers and their perceptions of you as the service provider will inevitably have an impact on your sales success. This chapter explains just why influencers make such formidable competitors.

KK: In Chapter 4, Deborah astutely identifies the government (or its legislation) as the "800-pound gorilla" versus service businesses. The perceptions of government being everywhere, yet still rather a somewhat unseen/unrecognized competitor, are dead-on.

CA: In deregulating U.S. telecommunications at the local level, for example, competitive advantage was derived as much by manipulating the regulatory environment as it was by traditional factors such as capabilities and pricing. The role of the government, both as a source of information, as well as a competitive factor, is often overlooked.

KK: In another instance, in my own field of information research, libraries offer fee-based services for businesses and are governmental competitors to my business.

RM: Knowing your competitors comes down to knowing their capabilities. However, Chapter 5 about traditional competitors discusses the issues that make this particularly challenging in the services sector.

JB: For example, in my area of the software business, where the largest firms have annual revenues of about $100 million and there are scores of small companies, identifying full and partial competitors can be a very elusive undertaking, especially where new entrants are concerned.

RM: The novel insight of this chapter suggests that a detailed understanding of your competitors will lead you to a comprehensive appreciation of your own services sector.

NS: The competitive landscape outlined in Chapter 6: An Inside Job is a favorite topic of mine. It is very common that clients, when requesting services, do not know or understand or appreciate the importance of determining their systemic or projected needs and matching those to the supplier.

BB: I was particularly reminded, while reading Chapter 6, of the three basic tenets of running a business, any business—ethics, innovation, and technology. As Deborah mentions, relying on past practice is a sure way to become a dinosaur. And far too many businesspeople today are caught up in technology for technology's sake and have forgotten business basics like strategy, planning, and innovation.

RM: Chapter 8: Where Are They? offers a systematic approach as well as helpful tips to finding your competitors. It is a common fallacy that we think we know where our competitors are, just because we live and breathe our business on a daily basis. Making this mistake leads to being blindsided by the competition.

CA: We've found it very important to keep an open mind when ferreting out new competitors or entering new markets. We have also found it very important to identify unique experts in the market you are exploring/playing in and to cultivate them through establishing a sense of mutual trust. This means thinking through what benefit the expert has in giving you information and making sure it is a win–win exchange for both parties.

NS: Being aware and sensitive to changes at the strategy level, as discussed in Chapter 9, or working backwards from the operational level to spot changes in the competition allows you to create a better identity and position. A thorough analysis revealing your competitors' basic thrust is imperative for your success. Yet in spite of this, I have had a couple of consulting experiences where I have done great homework, understood my competitors, and have lost to the competition because my firm is not a household name, even when we were told we provided the best proposal.

KK: Chapter 10: What Are They Selling?, like all of the other chapters, is written clearly and lucidly. Unfortunately, services do not fall under the conventional wisdom that "if it looks like a duck, walks like a duck, and quacks like a duck, it must be a duck."

BB: This chapter really struck home the importance of speaking with customers. Understanding what your competitors are selling is often a complex task, made even harder in the services sector. But your own firm's customers are a wealth of information, whether you are in manufacturing or services.

KK: And in Chapter 10, the reasons and methods for assessing your competitors' potential and services—basic, value-added, custom, and integrated—are provided in an easy-to-understand format.

JB: Chapter 11: The Marketing Challenge also looks at the importance of knowing how your competitors market—this can be a very effective sales tactic. As part of the sales cycle, we conduct win–loss analyses; from a competitive standpoint, the losses are particularly instructive. By contacting the company a few months after the decision has been made, it is also possible to find out how the competitor is doing; the follow-up may result in the re-establishment of a relationship.

CA: Chapter 14: All About Money introduces another important element; many companies don't understand their own costs, so it is often difficult for another company to assess true costs in a meaningful way. Cost determinants are often complex and, especially in the services industry, may not be linked with price. There are intangible elements such as perceptions of expertise and competence.

JB: Understanding who works for a competitor is essential. Chapter 15: Who Are They? discusses several sources for this kind of vital information, and it reminded me of the importance of profiling the sales and executive management team of key competitors.

NS: Knowing what clients want from their vendors allows you to feed into your strengths and position against the client's or competitor's weaknesses. Knowing the people, their capabilities, and their performance provides for you a mastery of your own human capital which you can turn into strategic and tactical advantage.

JB: One of our largest competing firms had grown very rapidly, but I was able to determine that almost half the employees had been hired in the past year. When talking to prospective customers, we would ask the question: Do you want a rookie running your implementation? The answer to that question is obvious!

NS: I know I am already looking forward to getting a whole copy of this book and seeing more of what Deborah has to offer.

KK: Overall, this book is an extremely value added read for anyone involved in a service business. And anyone interested in CI could pick up this book and be "one leg up" on the competition— almost instantly!

Introduction

"Competition is anything and everything which will send the dollars from your door." This is a phrase I have often used at seminars and presentations; I even use an overhead showing an animated building—your firm perhaps?—and a flock of winged dollar bills, rapidly vanishing over the horizon, leaving the building scratching its head!

It's important to consider the extent and scope of competition because not many companies, whether goods-producing or service-providing, want to countenance the diversity of competitive forces they face. Most people confine their examination of competition to just the other companies doing the same stuff that they are, what this book defines as traditional competitors or direct competitors. There are several reasons for this: traditional competitors are easy to spot; they are easy to study, especially the larger firms; and they allow for lots of nice, neat analyses.

Sadly, the real world bears no resemblance to this scenario; competition really and truly is "anything and everything" that will send the customers and thus their dollars *away from* your door. Competition can actually be the customers themselves, or it can be influencers who work at client or customer organizations. It can even be a third party like the government or—horrors!—it can be our very selves; more than one company has become adept at creating its own competition from within its four walls. Then there's a whole range of "left-field competition," which can arise out of nowhere and throw you flat on your back.

And nowhere is this diversity of competition more present than in the services sector. Unlike their goods-producing counterparts, service firms do not face "cut-and-dried" competition. Even worse, before now, no book has even looked at how you define and study competition in services or any sector where the output is not tangible but intangible. For this reason, I have made reference to the goods-producing sector from time to time as a way to illustrate the greater complexity of services competition and because anyone already familiar with competitive intelligence techniques has likely come across them solely in the context of products.

Oh, sure, most books on competitive intelligence do blithely toss around the phrase "products and services" but usually, by Chapter 3, the word "services" has dropped from view (although the author says that this is just for the sake of convenience and when the word "products" is used, "services" is really meant as well). But when you look at the methods and models these authors describe, you can quickly see there's no application in a service business. Most books, articles, conference papers, and case histories on competitive intelligence are applicable to products. All thoroughly explore ways to study head-counts, capacity utilization, throughput, shipments, raw materials, market penetration, and various other aspects of competing, which are just dandy if you're shipping widgets, but rarely, if ever, can these models and methods be used for services. They are not suited for studying how one law firm represents clients in court compared to another, how one recruiter finds the best candidates over another, how one consulting engineering firm can win more bids than another, how one market research firm can recruit better employees than another, or for analyzing the realities of the service, what comprises it and how it is delivered.

The closest many published works come to touching on services is by talking about hydroelectric services or telecom services; while these are certainly less tangible than automobiles or boxes of cereal, they're not always close enough (although this book does use examples from these sectors). Rather, this book talks about services where human labor with the value-added of expertise—intellectual capital—forms the core of the business.

To achieve this has been a tremendous challenge because there's a dearth of examples and case histories prepared by others. There are certainly few models to use in analyzing competition in services and, as a result, I have to say the book is very light on models. Many case studies were read, but few tackled the issues important to someone running a service business and wanting to study their competition. Some case histories from business schools talk about strategy in the loftiest terms but never touch ground and look at how to gather intelligence about this facet of a competitor. In other cases that study particular companies, there's a brief mention that Company ABC, when entering a particular market, faced competition from XYZ. And that's it. No details on how this competition was identified, no techniques on how to gather information about competitors, and no guidance on how to go ahead and analyze what is found.

So this book is, by its very nature, a start, a beginning, for more attention to be paid to competitive intelligence in services. In the first part of the book, I look at the varying forms of competition, both external and internal, that a service business might face, and which a company owner or manager needs to be aware of. I have particularly kept in mind that many service businesses are small and entrepreneurial or owner managed in nature, and even if they are growing, they are still not on a scale of, for example, the manufacturing or pharmaceutical industries. As a result, this book may not be of as much interest to the so-called Big Five management consulting firms, which are global in scope, or other similarly sized service firms. Not that there are that many, and given current trends, they'll soon all likely merge to form the Big One.

The second part of this book looks at traditional competitors, firms that claim to be offering what your firm does, and ways to study them. To this I must add a caution: there is no magic bullet. There is no one source to tap. There are no ready recipes for gathering intelligence about competitors and studying it. What I have provided are some ideas and the kind of thinking you need to undertake and the *types* of sources you need to tap to gather intelligence about traditional competitors. But there really is no definitive list of sources. Apart from other basic books about competitive intelligence (CI) on the market that do list some elementary sources, experience has shown me that each services sector, each company, needs its own sources and these need to be identified and developed organically, at the grass-roots level. So, I have instead tried to show the way to get people started.

As with all books, this one owes its existence to a collaborative effort, and so thanks are due to others. First, to John Bryans at Information Today, for taking an interest in the topic and working with me to develop the book. Then, thanks go to all the companies we have worked with since Information Plus was started in 1979; it is the assignments handled for them that have honed my understanding in the area of competitive issues in service businesses and, in some cases, given me examples to use in this book. Thanks also to the providers of various services who have shared their "war stories" with me and allowed these to be used as examples. The book would also have taken forever to put together if it had not been for the research assistance of Susan Hebdon, who ordered the case histories, visited the library, and tracked down often elusive background material for me to use. There would also be no manuscript for delivery to the publisher without the careful attention to detail of Linda Zangerle, who has labored, sometimes for entire days at a time, to get things in shape for shipping to the publisher.

And, finally, thanks to the times in which we live. Had it not been for our foremothers who have cleared the way for women to pursue more opportunities, it is unlikely I would have been able to neglect, albeit temporarily, so many of my "traditional duties" to devote myself to writing. Thanks also go to members of my family and to my friends who have, these last few weeks, been getting the message "don't call me, I'll call you" while I was in final stages of finishing the manuscript!

Deborah C. Sawyer
Buffalo, NY
August 2001

PART 1

THE

COMPETITIVE

LANDSCAPE

CHAPTER 1

Competitive Challenges for Service Businesses

Introduction

Once the forgotten stepchild of the manufacturing and industrial economy, the services sector has grown in importance over the last half of the 20th century until it now accounts for a sizeable percentage of the developed world's gross domestic product (GDP).

In the United States, services have grown from 68 percent of GNP—the measure then in use—in 1986 to more than 82 percent of GDP by 2000.[1, 2, 3] Employment in services has also kept pace; from 71 percent (1986) through 76 percent (1990) up to a total of 79 percent (1999).[1, 2, 4] Just as manufacturing and goods production transformed the established agrarian society over the last half of the 19th century, services have displaced industrial activity in the 20th. Even within the manufacturing sector, some 65–75 percent of employees perform service tasks such as research, logistics, maintenance, and design rather than make the goods.

Similar trends showing the growing role of services in the economy can be found in the countries of the European Union. As a percentage of GDP, Luxembourg enjoys the highest rate at 76 percent with the U.K. a close second at 73 percent.[4] Employment levels also show the importance of services, with countries like Sweden having 74 percent of its work force active in such businesses. Even countries that are still more agricultural show services labor participation rates well over the halfway mark, with Greece at 59 percent and Portugal at 60 percent.

Another forgotten aspect of services is that they are not as marginal in purchasers' hierarchies of needs as products, although the converse is generally held to be true. During recessions, consumers will often defer product purchases while continuing to make services purchases. Medical care, education, travel, and personal care do not necessarily represent choices that people can put off. Statistics show that the services sector as a whole does not suffer as much contraction during a recession as does the goods-producing sector.[1]

Given the obvious importance of services, why then do perceptions of services' marginality and lack of importance in the overall economy persist? Some of the reason, no doubt, rests in the nature of service businesses, which tend to be smaller in size, although large, global service firms do exist. Another reason is that services outputs are harder to measure and often involve subjective elements, such as goodwill, which does not lend itself to quantification.

These and additional factors, which will be discussed below, perhaps explain why there are also so few consistent definitions of just what is a service business. In fact, a search of business books, both famous and not-so-famous, indicates a lack of definitions, period. Even venerable classics, such as *In Search of Excellence*, do not even have the term "service business" or "service industry" in their indexes. Those books that do attempt some definition of services tend to offer discussions rather than precise, neat descriptions.

This lack of a definition or willingness to focus on the service business extends to the literature devoted to competition and competitive intelligence (CI). Most of the models, case studies, discussions, and research strategies recommended in these works focus on goods-producing businesses. Perhaps this is the final manifestation of the nature of service businesses; those involved in competitive intelligence want to avoid tackling the issue of CI precisely because the "beast" is untameable. It is much easier to discuss manufacturing and goods.

Defining the Service Business

Even books that do introduce the concept of competition in services do so only sparingly. Michael Porter, in his 1980 classic, *Competitive*

Strategy, has but four references to service industries in the index. From these we can glean some indication of how Porter defines a service business. He sees services as an industry that is fragmented, where no firm has significant market share nor can any one organization influence industry outcomes by setting the agenda for the industry (which does occur in goods-producing sectors, such as beer or steel, where one or two behemoths dominate). Such service industries he describes as being populated by a large number of small and medium-sized companies. Later in his book, Porter cites issues arising from where the service is performed, such as at the customer's premises or requiring the customer to come to where the service is produced, as further characteristics separating service businesses from goods-producing entities. The final characteristics are the close local or personal control of the ownership and the personal service, approach of the service provider.

This latter description is echoed by Ian Gordon in his book, *Beat the Competition*, where a service business is described as being characterized or differentiated on the basis of the service provider and the key role of relationship management. This changes the focus of competition for the service firm; factors such as recruitment of personnel and training may prove of greater significance in gaining competitive advantage than they would for a goods-producer; conversely, goods producers may be concerned about manufacturing throughput and capacity utilization, which have no relevance for the service firm.

Another facet of service business that helps define them is that they often deal with concepts and ideas. And concepts and ideas are easily replicated. Operators of service businesses do not have the protection of patents; at the very most, they can take out a trademark or servicemark on the name of a service or "package" of activities they have invented.

This particularly places the pioneers or innovators in services at a disadvantage. Those consultants who truly were the first to introduce the concept of Total Quality Management to the American marketplace soon found a host of copycats claiming to offer the same processes. Apart from any numerical competition this created, as more and more consulting firms jumped on the quality bandwagon, there was also the equal competitive threat of dilution or degradation of the service offering. It is one thing to say or advertise that you offer a quality process;

it is another to be able to deliver results. Botched delivery by another service provider who doesn't know what they're doing is just one aspect of services competition, as will be discussed later in Chapters 2 and 12. Another way of defining the services sector is that the key unit of inventory is time. As just about every adult learns, time is a valuable commodity and one that you can only spend in fixed amounts. From a business owner's point-of-view, it has an added liability because it cannot be stockpiled. Nor can it be returned and reused or resold; few service business owners have not had the experience of working on a project, providing a set number of hours to a client, only to have the client—for whatever reasons—refuse to pay their bill. Whereas in the goods sector, there is always the possibility, if the customer decides to return the merchandise, that it can be resold or the parts reused, there is no such option in services. Once you are in March, you cannot take back the first two weeks of February and resell them.

It is also possible to expand this facet of "time as inventory" and focus on time with the value-add of expertise. When we refer to a service business in this book, we mean any service based on human expertise, the input of human labor with the value-add of knowledge, brain power, or intellect. For our purposes, the types of service business we will be discussing in the case histories and other examples in the book include law firms, accounting firms, actuarial firms, management consulting firms, executive recruiters, marketing organizations, advertising and PR agencies, research companies, property management firms, energy auditors, investment/portfolio managers, economic forecasters, business brokers, and more. These are the types of business where, as ad man David Ogilvy once observed, "the inventory goes down in the elevator each night."

Foundations for Analysis

Given these various descriptions or definitions of a service firm, how can the manager or owner of such a business use this to better understand the environment in which he or she operates and therefore competes? By recognizing that certain realities will always be present and need to be reckoned with, the owner-operator or management team of a service firm can develop tools, solutions, and strategies to defend their existing business and find ways to use their knowledge to grow the business. The main tool for doing this is CI, although there are several specific challenges to face and overcome.

The services environment, as Michael Porter points out, will always be fragmented with multiple players, many of them small or even obscure. This immediately suggests that studying other providers—or traditional competitors—will be time consuming. The channels through which services are delivered—at the provider's location or the customer's—are nearly invisible to the outside observer and thus hard to study.

The pivotal nature of the relationship between provider and client and how this relationship is managed also goes on behind closed doors. It can be equally difficult to study customer service issues and how each service provider interacts with its customers, yet service levels and the rate of customer retention is a key factor in any service business' success.

The service itself tends to be elastic and readily tailored to suit each customer or client. This poses problems for analysis of competition because there may never be an exact match between services offered *within* a firm, never mind between firms. Most service providers of any longevity will have made it a practice to be flexible. One client may want a presentation and no report, another a report and no presentation. From day to day, each service firm adapts to meet the specific needs of its clients.

Marketing may also occur in private, by way of proposals or quotes, which never enter the public domain. Marketing may also be an entirely in-person phenomenon, dependent on the competing firm's personnel going out to call on prospective customers. There may never be any ads placed, there may be no Web site, there may not even be a brochure. Yet such a firm may have a wealth of business based on the most ancient and invisible marketing tactic of all, "word-of-mouth."

Other service providers may have different ways of managing their inventory (time) and different amounts of time to manage, distributed as it may be across a staff of full-time, part-time and freelance or contract workers, so studying this aspect of other service businesses can be challenging.

Then, within the scope of the value-added components, since services expertise rests with the individuals employed at a service provider, only by knowing the workers and their strengths and weaknesses can an assessment of the traditional competitor be made. Whereas in the goods-producing sector, it is possible to study the firm or company as an aggregate of its parts or people, in services, more needs to be known about the components or individuals that make up the total. Do all contract lawyers work at the same rate and produce the same results per hour? Do all executive recruiters interview the same number of candidates per day? The answer to these and similar questions is no, but these differences form an element of competition and need to be examined.

And, as if these factors were not enough of a challenge to study, there is the real *bête noir* of competitive intelligence gathering in the services sector: pricing. For many products, there are what are known as sticker or shelf prices, which are rarely negotiated. Even when the price of a product is negotiated, it usually rests on some factor such as quantity or turnaround time on delivery, which makes this facet of competition more visible and easier to study. Studying how a traditional competitor prices its services is extremely challenging because the service provider has full flexibility in adjusting its prices or presenting them in different ways to different customers. These issues will all be explored in Part 2 of the book.

How Services Competition Differs

Managers of service firms need to be aware of a broad spectrum of competitive factors, over and above the competition offered by other providers.

Many of these forces do not exist in the same degree in the goods-producing sector. A quick perusal of the CI literature quickly illustrates that studying competition in goods-producing sectors is very much a cut-and-dried affair. Goods-producing competitors are likely to be companies making the exact same item or making a very similar item; they will likely have a few defined locations and distribution channels with defined target markets and end-products. To see how this is so, think of what ends up on the shelves at the grocery store in the cereal section or what you find when you go to an auto aftermarket retailer for spark plugs. There is a certain standardization of product, the competition sits cheek by jowl on the shelves, it is easy to make comparisons; the customer can see, touch, smell, and even hear or taste the competitive offering. Similarly, the goods shipped direct from one manufacturer to the warehouse of another original equipment manufacturer (OEM) in the industrial sector are very cut-and-dried products.

Competition in service businesses is, instead, changing constantly, reminiscent of a kaleidoscope, with the sources of competitive threats shifting rapidly from customer or client to the next customer or client. There is no predicting which competitive forces you will necessarily face from day to day or week to week; differing competitive forces from one company you serve to another makes it far more difficult to study them. Generalizations are dangerous, as are assumptions. An open mind about the competition for each and every customer is essential. What this means, for the service business wishing to study its competition and undertake competitive intelligence, is an exercise in trying to hit a moving target.

The Broad Spectrum of Competitive Forces

As the competitive threats that often loom larger than threats from traditional competitors are discussed in detail in Part 1, this chapter will provide a brief overview. There are, first and foremost, the customers or clients themselves, who are often the biggest competitive threat in a service business and need to be studied as such. Then, there is a very troublesome group known as the influencer, a particularly important source of competition in businesses that serve other businesses or industries, government, and institutions. The influencer is not actually a purchaser but has a tremendous influence on the buying process; he can be a very negative force and a serious competitive threat. Then, there are competitive forces such as government itself, which may be providing services for free or on an at-cost basis in your markets; there is left-field competition, which is the surprise competition originating via new delivery channels such as the Internet, which can introduce competition located hundreds of miles from where you are actually operating; and then there is inside competition, competitive forces that originate internally at the company and thwart its growth. And, of course, there are the traditional competitors, companies that purport to provide the same or similar service to yours but may, in fact, be offering something quite different, but to which you are constantly compared.

Why Undertake CI in Services?

If studying services competition is so challenging and collecting intelligence about competitive forces so difficult, why undertake these activities at all? The reason is the reward from the effort involved: finding ways to gain competitive advantage.

While studies about competitive intelligence for services are few and far between, those that have been undertaken indicate a beneficial result for those services firms that conduct CI. Companies doing CI and offering both personal and business services tend to enjoy higher average sales than companies that do no CI; business services doing CI, in particular, enjoyed a greater market share than their counterparts that did not.[5]

As the economy globalizes and services themselves are exported and imported—a state of affairs unthinkable even 50 years ago—all operators of service businesses need to be more vigilant about existing and emerging competition, to both protect their existing business and to find ways to grow it.

Failing to study competition means failing to find ways to develop what's known as sustainable competitive advantage. By learning not only what your traditional competitors are up to but also finding out how they interact with the larger environment and all its competitive forces, a service business, however small, can become more adept at spotting opportunities. Similarly, by studying the various competitive threats originating with customers, influencers, from out in left field and more, the manager or owner of a service firm can become more proficient at seeing the threats and dealing with them before they capsize her company.

A Word About Words

Before moving into the in-depth discussion of services competition, a word about some expressions and terms used throughout the text is in order.

Clients. The preferred term for customers of a professional service firm. However, some definitions say a client is a customer who has become a client through repeated use of the service.

Customers. Customer is sometimes used to describe the purchaser of a product or of a "blue-collar service." But it also has the meaning of being a first-time user of a professional service (see *Clients* above). For this reason, and for sake of variety, these terms have been used interchangeably.

Direct Competition or Competitors. Another term for head-on competition or for traditional competitors.

Indirect Competition. A term used to describe a competitive force which does not compete head-to-head, but which fosters direct competition or facilitates it. Much government-origin competition falls into this category.

Influencers. Also referred to as buying influences, these people are not a direct purchaser or decision-maker but have input into the buying decision.

Primary Competition. This term is used to describe "front-line" competition, which may come from any or all of the sources discussed. (See *Secondary Competition*.)

Providers. Providers are all other companies that purport to provide the same services as you do. Not all providers are competitors. (See *Traditional Competitors*.)

Secondary Competition. This describes competition that is not in the front ranks. For example, if government influence or an economic recession with clients' budget cutbacks are the primary competition, then the traditional competitors are the secondary competition.

Single or Sole Source Supplier. Professional and similar services are often acquired without a bid or tender or other review of several providers. If a firm has specialized expertise, its services will be purchased on a "single source" or "sole source" supplier basis.

Traditional Competitors. The subset of providers who do compete against you.

References

1. "Will Services Follow Manufacturing Into Decline?" *Harvard Business Review*. November-December 1986: 95-103.
2. "Beyond Products: Services-Based Strategy." *Harvard Business Review*. March-April 1990: 58-67.
3. "Jobs: How Long Can Services Pick Up The Slack?" *Business Week*. February 19, 2001: 34-35.
4. *"The World Fact Book*. CIA, 2000.
5. "A Link Between CI & Performance." *Competitive Intelligence Review*. Summer 1995: 16, 18, 20.

CHAPTER 2

Customer-Origin Competition

While traditional competitors (companies providing the same or similar products) form the bulk of competition in goods-producing industries, for service businesses the biggest source of competition—and the most easily overlooked—is the customer. Customers are a form of competition that has been recognized for some time,[1] but this element of competition is still not given full attention by companies in service industries. Perhaps it has elements of *Et tu Brute,* a case of too cruel a thought? In service industries, the tendency is to see customers or clients as partners, allies, not entities against which one competes. To think adversely about customers is almost a sacrilege, so strong is the indoctrination in business schools, how-to books for entrepreneurs, and customer service seminars for businesspeople over the importance of the customer.

The True Arena of Competition

There are many reasons this position is a dangerous one; in just about every industry, the customer's mind is the true arena of competition. It is here that comparisons are made, suppliers chosen or eliminated, and other decisions affecting the purchase of services made. It is also in the customer's mind that budgets are allocated to different suppliers and may even be shifted to quite dissimilar services from the ones your company provides. Although in many cases it may *seem* as if the traditional competitors are the source of competition, this is merely an illusion. How customers make their decisions may have little relation to the tactics a traditional competitor might be employing (although the role of traditional competitors in the marketplace will be discussed in Chapter 5).

The Role of Prior Relationships

Another reason that customers or clients figure so strongly in service industry competition is that the role of the relationship between supplier and customer is much stronger than in a goods-producing industry. Beyond the relationship between clients and your traditional competitors, it is the customer's or client's emotional experience of the relationship that weighs most heavily on how they go about selecting a supplier. The mere existence of a prior relationship may be enough to preclude consideration of any other options. Consider this small anecdote about the choice of a supplier for an access control system at the Canterra Tower in Calgary, Canada. The existing system, which was literally falling apart, had to be replaced, so the general manager of the property received approval to go to the marketplace for a proposal to install a new access control system. But instead of actually seeking proposals from several possible suppliers or reviewing all the options available, the building management instead went with Johnson Controls. Why was this choice made? What key attribute directed this piece of business to this supplier? It seems Johnson Controls had recently purchased a security company, Card Key Systems. The story in *Security Magazine*[2] reports: "Because of their favorable relationship with Johnson Controls, the Canterra Tower chose the Card Key System." Was the Card Key System necessarily the best on the market? Was it necessarily the most cost-effective? The article does not say, but the mere presence of an existing or prior relationship seems to have been the deciding factor in the purchase.

This suggests that service businesses, which want to keep abreast of their competition and be able to study it fully, need to keep on top of exactly who customers look at when they first sit down to make any kind of supplier decision. It is equally important to remember that who customers look at may not meet *your* definition of competition; you may find your own company, regardless of what you supply, "lumped in" with a range of other services that seem to bear little or no resemblance to yours.

Competition from Alternates and Substitutes

Such situations occur because those who choose to purchase services may be in a position to choose between alternates in meeting their needs, alternates being options *within* a sector that enable the purchaser to get the job done. There are many companies that designate themselves market research firms, but the work they do, the methodologies they use, and the outputs they produce can vary tremendously. A firm that conducts only telephone research may therefore find itself frequently compared to one that utilizes focus groups exclusively, while both may be compared to the research available from either a public relations firm or an advertising agency; such agencies will provide additional value-added services that the pure research companies alone cannot provide. Seeing this many dissimilar competitors in the picture does not fit with the neat, conventional models of competition used in the goods-producing sector, but it is exactly the sort of competitive landscape where service businesses compete.

In the arena of legal services, such alternates are found in Do-It-Yourself (D-I-Y) will packages, which obviate the need for the in-person services of a lawyer. Providers of consulting services may find their high-end offering competing with what's known as an "off-the-shelf" report, which may cost only a few hundred dollars rather than the thousands a consultant charges to prepare a custom study.

In addition to alternates, a competitive threat that originates among the customers is that of substitutes, where firms operating in quite different industries may be played off one against the other. Providers of substitutes, who suddenly appear on the radar screen of a service business, are usually companies from *outside* the industry. This introduces the element of indirect competition into the mix, creating a much larger competitive playing field. No industry is immune to this form of competition, but few recognize it. One organization that does is Blockbuster Video, which acknowledges that they are not just competing against other video stores but against wherever and however customers spend their entertainment dollars.

The financial services industry offers an illustration of how broad the substitute form of competition can be. Although most banks consider other banks the competition, in reality, traditional banking services (often referred to as transaction banking) may be available from brokerage houses, credit unions, financial planners, insurance companies, and accountants. In the arena of services available for financing purchases, as well as traditional lenders, retail stores offer their own financing and thus a form of competition to the banks. So do car dealers for automobile purchases. It was precisely the issue of substitutes that had to be recognized and dealt with by Investore, the retail money management concept introduced a few years ago by Bank of Montreal. As well as traditional lenders, the bank had to consider how much competition would originate from virtual financial institutions, such as ING Direct, and companies like Schwab. Even software companies, such as Microsoft, offer solutions that customers can substitute for the money management services available from banks.[3]

In a similar fashion, Southwest Airlines was able to build its business by understanding the real source of its competition. Such competition, the airline realized, did not originate with other airlines—the traditional competitors—but with a range of other short-haul transportation options, such as self-drive cars, rental cars, trains, and buses. All represented substitutes to taking a plane for short trips and all represented various options for individuals' travel needs.[4] In looking for solutions, customers are less concerned about who provides them and have no interest in whether or not they restrict their choice to a narrow range of competing companies designated as such by your firm. It is only by recognizing who your customers or clients see as offering a parallel or substitute to you that you can hope to gain mastery over the competition.

Competing Against a Lack of Action

Another dimension of this customer-origin competition is the customer's own inaction. Many service firms have had the experience of submitting a quote or proposal and then finding the customer takes no action. Rather than the customer, or client in this case, choosing to go ahead with someone else, it may simply be that they cannot make up their minds and so are doing nothing. Or, they may not wish to spend the money involved in going ahead with anyone; services in general are still viewed as a "soft cost" at many companies and, whereas these organizations cannot risk scrimping on aspects of production, they can always justify saving money by not purchasing services at all. Related to this is the role budget cutbacks will often play in the decision to use a service or not. Again, the lack of money at a client company is not something your traditional competitors have engineered; furthermore, they will suffer equally with you if the clients have no money. Rather, the lack of an appropriate budget is the source of the competitive threat and thus originates directly with and is under the control of the customer.

A lack of willingness to take action, combined with budget issues, were just two of the factors conspiring against the use of a security consultant by Genuity Inc., a major ISP/network firm. Genuity had initiated contact with the security consultant and the director of corporate security had asked for a proposal. On receipt of this document, interest remained strong in trying out the consultant's proposed ideas, likely as a pilot project. However, a strike temporarily disrupted normal business activities; once this was settled, the director of corporate security had a new hire, a security manager, a direct report to him, who would now quarterback the work outlined in the proposal. The consultant began following up with this individual, only to hear versions of "don't call us, we'll call you." The original interest and conviction of the need for the service on the part of the director was not mirrored in the new person. Since going back to speak to the director was not "politically correct," because it would involve going behind the security manager's back, the consultant ended up in "no man's land" without this particular piece of work. At no time, however, had another provider (a traditional competitor) entered the picture, because this particular consultant had a unique offering. Instead, customer-origin competition was at work.

Reluctance to Change as Competition

The customer's reluctance to change and try out a new supplier can be a sizeable form of competition to new market entrants as well as established services suppliers who are interested in expanding their market share. If a prospective client or customer already has existing suppliers, what some refer to as "the usual suspects," breaking through this barrier can be extremely difficult. However, the customer's reluctance to change is in no way a measure that traditional competitors have found successful tactics to keep you out of the market. In fact, in this scenario, the established suppliers may have become very lazy and may not be doing a particularly good job. What you are competing against here is the customer's inability to plan ahead and find time to implement change by way of introducing new suppliers. Even when companies do go out for proposals from two or three suppliers before awarding a piece of business, the frequent answer, heard by any non-established suppliers as to why their bid was not successful, is that the decision has been made in favor of a known entity. This was the scenario that greeted a financial consulting firm, which had been requested to submit a bid to Household Finance Corporation. The firm was excited by the chance to land a new client but, after all the bids were in, the decision was made in favor of the incumbent. The coordinator handling the proposals explained it this way: "Oh, our Vice President knew this other firm and so he felt most comfortable with them." The fact that the chosen supplier with the inside track had been two weeks late with their bid did not influence the outcome. Note also that the work to be performed, the qualifications of the bidding firms, and any kind of rational process to select the *correct* supplier, did not really enter into the decision.

The Do-It-Yourself Phenomenon

Customers in service businesses can also pose a competitive threat via their desire to do everything themselves. One of the dangers in a line of work where you have to frequently spell out, in a proposal or quote, exactly what it is you are going to do, is that this approach puts your cards too firmly on the table and leads to scenarios where customers think to themselves, "Oh, if that's all that's involved, we can do that ourselves." Such competition often originates with junior staff members who want to prove themselves and who step forward with an "I can do that" attitude about the service to be performed. This is particularly true for services where there are no formal or agreed-upon qualifications, which is true of many services. It is less likely that this would happen with a legal or accounting service, where a professional designation may be mandatory to handle the work.

This D-I-Y form of competition was at work when a consultant in the customer service business was approached by Dictaphone, a manufacturer of dictation and other office equipment, to undertake some segment research. According to the consultant, Dictaphone understood the industrial segment but needed to know more about retail channels that served students and consumers with their products as well as the commercial segment (offices and the like). The consultant therefore prepared a proposal, outlining what steps would be undertaken and the methods to be used to investigate these market segments.

The contact at Dictaphone, the VP of Sales, received the proposal and then called the consultant back. According to this individual: "We now have a good handle on the retail segment," so a revised proposal was called for, focusing solely on the commercial segment. The composition of "we" was not specified, but it was hinted that this was the senior management group.

A second proposal was therefore submitted and, after an eight-week delay, a go-ahead was given. The consultant therefore began work investigating customer service satisfaction in the subsegments within the commercial market (e.g., general offices, doctors and other medical facilities, legal firms, etc.).

Work was only one-third of the way along when the VP of Sales called again and suggested Dictaphone now knew about most of these segments and wished to revise the work even further, to scale back the project. After dickering over budgets, an agreement was reached for the final thrust of the research and the consultant proceeded.

It was only another week before the VP of Sales called again to say the company now knew about all its markets and wished to put a halt to the work. The consultant was left "holding the bag" and had to threaten legal action to get paid for the work that had been done. What the consultant was really competing against here was the company's internal impetus to do the research itself.

Another form that D-I-Y competition takes occurs when a long-established policy of outsourcing undergoes a major change and client or customer organizations decide to bring certain services in-house. This can affect service providers in many sectors: travel agencies, printers, graphic designers, market researchers, recruiters, law firms, and more.

Too Much Competition

If the true arena of competition is the customer's mind, this will be doubly true in cases where there seems to be too much competition, making the customer's choice a difficult one. This happens in services sectors such as management consulting, which is a vague enough term to cover a whole range of offerings including, but not limited to, executive search, change management, IT and automation, knowledge management, quality programs, and more. Faced with such an abundance, the customer or client becomes paralyzed and sees the situation as fraught with hazard, in that it would be much easier to pick the wrong consultant when there is too much competition than to pick the right one. Services such as long-distance telephone and cell phone plans are also exemplars of this problem, where the range of providers, along with multiplicity of plans available, are enough to confuse anyone and put someone off making a decision, due to the overwhelming nature of the task and the time required to make a choice. Financial services, particularly investing in mutual funds, is another example. At one time, there were only a few dozen mutual funds; now, it seems, there are thousands. This overwhelming array of choice leads to inertia on the part of customers which, in turn, creates a sizeable competitive threat in the marketplace.

Bad Experiences

Related to this is the way customers stick with no "suspects" at all because their prior contact, with professional services firms, colors their willingness to make further purchases. This may create competitive barriers, even when what you offer is quite different from what caused the customer's negative experiences. If customers perceive they did not get value for money or that very little was provided for the fees charged or they were not able to use the results with the consultant they hired, they will tend to magnify this experience to encompass any and all providers of services.

A provider of online database search services encountered such perceptual barriers in the president of a cosmetics packager start-up known as OPM Cosmetics. The president of OPM wanted to obtain certain market statistics from online searches but, prior to going ahead, wanted to get a report back from an industrial designer the firm had commissioned to advise on packaging and related issues.

When the sales representative from the database search firm phoned OPM Cosmetics back, as agreed, she found a distraught president and no business for her own firm. As the president explained: "We paid this guy $1,500 and I can't believe how little work he has done, I'm just disgusted." Apologizing for having to back out of the online search work, the President explained that the experience with the industrial designer had led her to re-evaluate all use of outside services; as a start-up, her company didn't have money to burn. In this case, what kept a piece of business and thus revenue from the database search provider was not the actions of another database service but those of a consultant in an entirely different line of work. But such is the nature of services competition that a "bad apple" in one sector can spoil things for consultants in many other sectors and thus create a competitive barrier to growth.

Once the customer has been burned by a less-than-perfect supplier, she may be reluctant to risk any repeat experiences, even though the service in question might be of value to the organization. This can apply to purchases along the whole spectrum of services from maintenance and delivery services, through research services, printing and design, and on to advertising and public relations, and recruitment services.

The Need for Education

Another element that needs to be factored into a study of competition in the services sector is the role a customer's lack of knowledge has to play. If the service you are offering is new, many prospective customers or clients may never have heard of it. This is going to exert a far greater competitive barrier to growth than anything a provider of something similar, such as a traditional competitor, might do. When your service is truly new enough, you may not even have traditional competitors. If customers do not know what it is you do, have never seen an output, and are not sure what they would be getting for their money, then long before any relationship can be established, a process of education must occur to bring customers or clients up to speed.

Education may also play a role if customer perceptions are completely at odds with the reality of the marketplace. This is particularly true around issues of price where people tend to forget that price is what you pay while performance is what you buy. A law firm offering services at rates much higher than their peers is not necessarily better and may even be worse in the role of counsel. Forgetting that it is the performance of the lawyer and the reliability of their advice, which is of paramount importance, occurs when customers focus solely on the price. Similarly, in the arena of travel services, a cut rate fare on an airline is not of much use if the airline in question has only one plane and that plane breaks down, stranding you at some airport not serviced by any other airlines.

That the role of client education is important is shown by this tale. A financial services firm, well established nationwide and providing retirement and other investment counseling to individuals, decided it should understand its competition better. In consultation with a leading CI association, it identified firms to whom it could send a request for proposal (RFP).

A CI consulting firm decided to submit a proposal and contacted the investment firm to obtain more information about what was required. Detailed discussion occurred; the consultant also asked the names of the other firms to whom proposal requests had been sent and discovered there were four firms, all of which were known to the consultant.

The consultant submitted a very detailed proposal and did so by the due date for delivery of proposals. On phoning the following week, to determine the status of the proposals and when a decision might be reached, the CI consulting firm found out that other firms had not submitted in time and had been granted an extension. No notification of such an extension had been sent to the CI consultant. More time passed and the consultant again followed up with the contact at the financial services firm. The consultant was told that no decision had yet been made but one was expected soon. The consultant obtained a date for a suitable callback and committed to doing so with the client.

When the time came to call back, the CI consultant reached the contact at the financial services firm and was told the project had been awarded to another firm. On asking which firm had been selected to do the CI work, the contact mentioned a firm with a name totally unfamiliar to the CI consultant. This firm had not been on the list of firms provided at the start of the bidding process. When probed about who this firm was and their track record in CI, it turned out to be a public relations firm that the investment company had worked with for two or three years. On asking how much experience this PR firm had with doing CI, the contact cheerfully advised: "Oh, none!" The fact that an inexperienced firm might do a lot of damage did not seem to have occurred to this company. It also indicated they could benefit from more education!

Location as Perceptual Competition

As if steering through this minefield of customer-origin competition is not enough, there is another element to consider: how your location affects your customers' perceptions. A management consulting firm, based in Western New York, undertook a sizeable project for Intertek Testing Services, based in New England. The work completed was pronounced satisfactory but, after this initial project, the consultant could not land any more business from Intertek.

By keeping in touch, the consultant began to unravel the reasons. Located close to the consultant's office was another testing service, ACTS, a competitor to Intertek. Although the management consulting firm did no work for ACTS—in fact, had no contact with the organization whatsoever—Intertek developed a perceptual problem around the proximity of its one-time consultant to a rival testing lab. For this reason, Intertek never again placed business with the firm.

While madly relocating around the country is no answer to such a situation, if your reassurances to a client or prospective client are not enough to overcome their fears, their perceptions about your location will linger as a more formidable competitive barrier than any actions by a traditional competitor.

Market Cooperation

So far, all the examples of customer-origin competition apply to the one-on-one situation, involving just one services supplier and one customer or client. But what about customers in aggregate? What does a mass movement by the customers do to competition?

During recessionary times, for example, all your customers may lack budgets; while it is true your firm and the other traditional competitors may be competing with one another for a reduced "pie," the broader competition to be faced is the slowdown in the economy. (This type of broader competitive factor will be explored in Chapter 7 about left-field competition.)

Sometimes these mass movements are referred to as "market cooperation" and they need to be examined carefully. Not being fully aware of the possibility of a mass exodus of customers created some problems for WFNX-101.7 FM. Perceived as the "station of the young," WFNX-101.7 FM thought it had a "lock" on the market for alternative rock in Boston. The aftermath of a local concert that had been well attended saw many other area radio stations start playing the same music, which led to a substantial exodus of once-loyal listeners of WFNX. Once this trend had been identified, the station's owners were in a position to deal with their new competition, which came from two directions: the actions of traditional competitors and of customers who had ceased to "cooperate."[5]

Tackling Customer-Origin Competition

One of the best ways to tackle competition emanating from customers or clients is simply to be aware it exists and keep in touch with your customers. More detailed discussion of how to keep on top of competition by way of competitive intelligence gathering will be found in Part 2 of this book, although some obvious measures can be stated here. Keeping in the loop, either by making sure your firm is on customers' mailing lists or setting up scanning or monitoring services (to truly be effective, both paper-based as well as electronic channels need to be used) are common sense measures.

Although a program designed to keep you in the know about customers is one of the more effective CI measures, it alone is not enough. Before leaving customers or clients aside, it is essential to look at their "twin," the influencer, who sometimes lurks inside a customer organization, sometimes without, and which will be explored in Chapter 3.

References

1. *Competitive Strategy*. 1980 ed.: 6.
2. "Multi-tenant Retrofit Saves Time, Money." *Security Magazine*. August 2000: 24.
3. "Bank of Montreal: Investore." Ivey Management Services. 1999: 23.
4. "Substitutes: Your Next Marketing Headache." *Competitive Intelligence Magazine*. April-June 1998: 44-46.
5. "WFNX-101.7 FM and Boston's Radio Wars." Babson College. 1999: 28.

Competition Checklist

Here are the key questions to ask yourself to determine the role customer-origin competition plays in your business.

✔ Are you frequently the sole supplier considered for a piece of business that you do not land?

✔ Are there only a handful of other providers (traditional competitors) operating in your markets?

✔ Are you frequently asked to submit proposals or quotes to meet a customer's or client's requirements for three quotes?

✔ Are you frequently the "other guy" considered when you know the customer/client has a long-established supplier relationship with another firm?

✔ Are there so many traditional competitors operating in your markets that it is hard to track them all or what they offer?

✔ Is there more than one way to solve the problem your customer/client has?

✔ Do your customers/clients regularly take weeks to decide about going ahead with work that is supposedly urgent?

✔ Have your customers/clients ever made skeptical or even derogatory remarks about other service providers?

✔ Have you ever submitted a quote or proposal to a particular client and had no feedback from them, only to learn later they did the work themselves?

✔ Are there frequently changes in the incumbents in the functions or positions you deal with at your customers/clients?

Key Points to Remember

☛ Making the shift to seeing customers as "frontline" competition rests on understanding the psychology of individual decision-makers; their tendencies to take no action; their reluctance to change; their clinging to bad experiences, etc.

☛ Misdiagnosing customer-origin competition is also easy. The actions of traditional competitors may not be keeping business away from you; the customer's laziness or unwillingness to try new suppliers may be the real stumbling block.

☛ The longer another provider has had a relationship with a client or customer, the more entrenched the customer-origin competition will be.

☛ Customer-origin competition can arise very quickly; the biggest triggers are personnel changes or budget cutbacks.

☛ The less real authority decision-makers at a client company have, the more they will prove a source of competition.

CHAPTER 3

A Matter of Influence

Unseen, and often unstudied, are the influencers who form an equally sizeable competitive threat in service businesses. If customers—who generally are the decision-makers you deal with directly—represent a formidable opponent at times, then influencers—who may be the decision-makers' colleagues, supervisors or other consultants working with the company—run them a close second and may, in some sectors, even surpass them as a threat. Influencers are everywhere at an organization and may become involved in purchase decisions by suggesting the need for a service, by establishing specifications, evaluating suppliers, recommending or suggesting suppliers, or approving, authorizing, or making the final purchase. They can influence the choice of supplier by using persuasion or more strenuous tactics for a range of services including accounting, advertising, PR, promotion and incentives, banking, design and engineering, consulting, meetings, training, delivery and shipping, investments, health benefits, legal services, telecommunications, printing, insurance, real estate, security services, temporary help, travel, and more.

What is particularly troublesome about their presence is that their influence may be subjective; whereas, in goods-producing businesses, a product is simply a product, such clarity or definition eludes the procurement of many services. For example, if a company needs new filters for its equipment, then it buys new filters. And it has to buy those that fit its equipment. There's no debate. If the wrong type of paper will jam the printing presses, then only the appropriate paper will be purchased. If the truck needs new tires, only those rated for the weight and class of vehicle will be considered. In the business-to-business arena, subjective influencer activity is unlikely to show up over the purchase of products.

Spotting Centers of Influence

This is not the case with services, and influencers are the people who can sway a purchase decision from one supplier to another for completely irrational and biased reasons. Consider this example from the health insurance field. The benefits manager for a large manufacturer in Pennsylvania, while being interviewed a few years ago about group health insurance and the various carriers operating in her state, revealed: "I've only been here a year, but as soon as I arrived, I set to work to change this company over to U.S. Health." This carrier is now the manufacturer's sole insurer. This was not a bad development for U.S. Health, but what about the previous supplier, Capital Blue Cross, which had served the account faithfully for 10 years? No doubt, the folks at Capital Blue Cross, when told their contract would not be renewed, went off to "lick their wounds" and then spent some time analyzing the merits and demerits of U.S. Health as a competitor, believing that an aggressive marketing effort or cut-rate pricing by this carrier had lost them the contract with the manufacturer. But what really occurred was that Capital Blue Cross had been unseated not by traditional competitive forces, but by a center of influence. Their performance as the manufacturer's insurer may not have been at fault but this may never have entered consideration; the benefits manager's personal prejudices had had everything to do with their loss of the business.

Competing against such a force is very difficult, but all service businesses need to take it into consideration. The other problem with the center of influence is that it does not always reside in expected areas; in service industries, even when the services are contract-based, the purchasing department or official buyers may not have a very strong role in the supplier decision. Services are frequently contracted for, far away from established procurement channels. This means any number of departments in an organization, from operations or manufacturing through to marketing and advertising and on up to the executive suite, can be the home of a center of influence. Such centers of influence may actually be prior incumbents in decision-maker positions where, for example, they purchased marketing or advertising services, but such individuals have now moved on to other positions at the company. Such prior incumbents may have favorites among the supplier base and may therefore work to influence the new incumbent in their old position to continue to select the existing suppliers. When such new incumbents are not strong decision-makers, they are much more likely to be beset by a center of influence.

Such transitions can work the other way, when an influencer moves closer to the "hot seat" of decision-making. A consultant undertook a project for the Optical Products Division of Leica Incorporated. When the work was completed, the company's marketing director exclaimed: "This is one of the best consulting reports I have ever seen!" Such acclaim boded well for an ongoing business relationship.

But a few months later, the marketing director left and one of the product managers took over the position. The consultant, in the spirit of good client relations, followed up with the new incumbent, who had been at the presentation from the earlier work and had been one of the beneficiaries of the results. What a difference the passage of time had wrought! The new director panned the consultant's work and could not say enough bad things about it. The consultant was baffled until a chance encounter with the former director cleared things up. "I'm sorry to hear that," he explained, "but Vic never liked me and so, by association, he doesn't like any of the suppliers I had selected." Irrational behavior? Yes. Biased? Yes. But that is not uncommon in services and shows how those operating such businesses need to be aware of how influencers feel and think in addition to keeping tabs on the principal customer contacts.

Decision by Committee

Another factor creating the influencer as a competitive force is the trend in many organizations to flatter hierarchies and consensual decision-making. Rather than allowing one or two individuals to make a decision, several people at the organization are supposed to have input, which tends to dilute the focus of the decision and introduce a lot of random factors into the discussion process. This may be a particularly prevalent practice at smaller, entrepreneurial organizations or at those with employee-owners. For example, if a company had been about to contract with an outside supplier of training seminars, such as for quality processes or motivational services, consensual decision-making, where a range of influencers enter the fray, may lead the company to decide not to spend its money on either of those things and instead hire an individual on staff to perform these tasks or spend their money elsewhere on a substitute, such as a promotional brochure or an additional Web site. To hark back to the discussion in Chapter 2, it is easy to see now how this influencer factor works with customer-origin competition, to muddy the picture for anyone trying to analyze their competition in a service business.

Of course, there are times when this influencer factor creates a positive outcome, even during bid situations that are reviewed by committee. A market research company received a call, out of the blue, from a pharmaceutical firm they had never done business with before. Discussion ensued, a proposal was submitted and, within 24 hours, the research company had a new piece of business. At this point, they considered asking their contact, "How did you hear about us?" as being, perhaps, too much a case of "biting the hand that feeds." It was only the next day, when the market research firm received an e-mail that they solved the puzzle. There was, indeed, an influencer at work, behind the scenes; a former client, who had changed jobs a few months prior and knew the firm's work, had obviously been nudging the bid in his old supplier's favor.

Delegation as a Competitive Barrier

In organizations where there are still defined chains of command, the structure itself can create a further competitive factor. Let us suppose a provider of database management services or executive recruitment has been in to visit a decision-maker somewhere in the chain of command at a particular company. This could be a middle manager, someone lower down, or even a vice president at the executive level. This individual likes the services and sees value in them, but decides that a subordinate—or on occasion, a superior—is the best person to actually go ahead and implement use of the services. Delegation occurs and the service provider quickly finds itself in a position of "spinning its wheels." The initial contact, who is highly enthusiastic and saw great potential in the service, in spite of communicating this to their colleague, is quickly out of the picture. And it soon becomes apparent that the individual now responsible for making the decision and working with the services supplier sees no value whatsoever in what is being offered and plans to stall the decision indefinitely.

No matter that the company to whom the services were offered may be in dire need of a new security system, for example, or a better recruitment advisor, or some outsourcing of an unwieldy database. These issues do not enter the picture. But from the service provider's point-of-view, the "chain of command" as influencer has once again exerted a competitive force to stall the growth of their own business.

This influencer activity will likely forever impede the relationship between a pharmaceutical manufacturing company based in Minnesota and a consulting firm offering services to the industry. One of the firm's consultants met the manufacturer's Vice President of Regulatory Affairs at the Drug Information Association annual meeting in San Diego. The VP was very interested in the scope of services the consulting firm offered and asked for follow-up; once the VP had the consultant's prospectus, he suggested an in-person presentation to the team was in order.

The meeting was duly arranged, with two vice presidents, a regulatory affairs manager, a product manager, and the director of market research in attendance. Everything went well until the Q&A part of the presentation, whereupon the director of market research started to cast aspersion on the consultant's ethics. The consultant addressed the concerns raised, only to have the director of market research exclaim: "Well, we're already well served by consultants." He then stomped out of the meeting. Meanwhile, the two VPs stayed to chat with the consultant. "I don't agree with George," one stated. "We can always use more suppliers who offer what you do." Although the meeting ended in agreement to "keep in touch," the presence of a negative influencer like George at this manufacturing company will likely represent a considerable barrier—and competitive threat—to the consulting firm. To consider that the manufacturer's existing suppliers are the competitive factor is to "bark up the wrong tree"—the actions of an influencer like George weigh more heavily and are the more serious threat.

Recognizing the Role of Gatekeepers

Internal influencers based at a customer's site aren't the only type of influencer a service provider has to contend with. External influencers or "gatekeepers" who refer business or bring two other parties together to do business represent another facet of this aspect of competition.

A market research services firm received a call in November from a contact at an ad agency, asking the market research firm to put in a proposal for one of the ad agency's clients, Carrier. Carrier had long been in the business of manufacturing air conditioning equipment but, sensing some stagnation in market share growth for its traditional markets, wanted to diversify by adding services to offer duct cleaning. The company therefore wanted a report discussing the size of the market, who competed in duct cleaning, the size of the firms, their reputation, how they packaged or bundled their services, their pricing, the customers, etc. According to the ad agency, this new undertaking was a high priority for the company. The ad agency contact also told the consultant that their firm was the only one being asked to bid.

The consultant sent in a proposal very promptly to the ad agency; calls were placed to make sure the proposal had been received. (It had.) How did it look? (Fine.) How was the price? (Okay.) The ad agency said it had not yet had a chance to forward this to Carrier but would be doing so the following week. Everything looked good.

In December, prior to the Christmas break, the consultant followed up with the ad agency contact. There had been no decision yet and the client would likely want to wait until the new year to go forward. However, it was still a high priority for the A/C manufacturer.

In January, the consultant followed up again. According to the ad agency contact, there was no word yet but the project may now not be as high a priority as once believed. The consultant asked pointedly about any other bids and was told by the contact at the ad agency: No, yours is the only proposal they are looking at.

Time passed. About two months later, the consultant phoned the ad agency contact again and eventually got a callback saying that the project had been shelved. With the contact at the ad agency acting as a gatekeeper, the consulting firm had no opportunity to speak directly with Carrier. Nor did they know who at Carrier was the decision-maker; this was information the ad agency refused to divulge. There was no opportunity to communicate directly, which usually allows for the services provider to answer questions and clear the way for a go-ahead. Perhaps Carrier had concerns about value for money? The reliability of the results? Confidentiality issues? What is also not known is the ad agency's agenda: perhaps it worked to divert money set aside for the business expansion to its own services, cutting the consulting firm out? With gatekeeper influencers, any or all of these scenarios are possible. Recognizing that they are a competitive factor allows you to decide how to deal with them—or if you even want to deal with them at all. It may be a better strategy to focus on business opportunities that are not under the control of a gatekeeper.

Managing Multiple Influencers

If one or two internal influencers seem troublesome, imagine if your client companies are just riddled with them and that they all have input into decisions about your services. This competitive threat is actually two-edged: on the one hand, there are more people than ever to slow down a decision, divert funds to substitutes or alternates, cry foul of using outside suppliers due to bad experiences in the past, or make a case for "the usual suspects." On the other hand, landing a piece of business with such an organization will require a far greater input of your time beforehand to educate all these buying influences than would be required for a company with a single decision-maker.

It was recognition of this influencer factor and the need to assess knowledge levels and the possible need for customer education that led London Life Insurance Company to speak at length with financial controllers and other parties in the 250–500 lives size-band, the insurance industry's way of describing companies with 250 up to 500 employees. London Life had the suspicion that such customers were in a position to self-insure for at least part of their coverage and so wanted to offer a service that offered design innovations. What London Life needed to find out was the extent to which such companies were willing to trade off design and cost while absorbing more risk. The investigation showed influencers at each customer were distributed across a spectrum from those who understood the concept completely to those who failed to grasp it. In this way, the insurer was able to prepare accordingly before it rolled out its new product. Had it not known the trouble spots, a backlash of influencer misunderstanding could have capsized the service before it had time to establish itself.

In some sectors, there may be a multitude of external gatekeepers or influencers to reckon with. This was the situation facing National Fuel Gas a few years ago. Knowing that energy services decisions in the construction industry often swung between gas, electricity, and newer sources of energy, such as propane or options such as cogeneration, National Fuel wanted to get beyond the decision-makers and corral the influencers—the architects, engineers, contractors, and other professionals—who could sway the energy decision on both new and retrofit projects. To do this, the firm built a database; to enhance the value of this tool even more, relationships *between* influencers, such as engineers and architects who frequently worked together on projects, were also identified and entered into the database.

What this exercise revealed was a web of contacts throughout National Fuel's service territory that could effectively wield influence over most of the ultimate decision-makers in the commercial construction sector. For National Fuel to counteract this form of competition, as well as marketing and promoting the benefits of gas to the decision-makers (the customers), the company also had to set up programs specifically designed to target and reach the influencers and educate them about its services.

Tackling Influencer Competition

If you take the steps outlined in Chapter 2 to keep abreast of customer-origin competition, you'll already have much of the foundation for keeping on top of internal influencer competitive forces. An additional step to take, however, is to set up a system for checking internal promotions that create new influencers at your customers, and of identifying who works with, for, and above your primary client contacts. These people can prove valuable links for combatting influencer competition if your contact leaves the company.

With external influencers, you will need to assess how many there are and if you need to set up a formal tool such as a database to monitor their relationships and where they have influence. As for gatekeeper influencers who act as a competitive barrier at times, the best approach is to study their track record with you. If they ask for a lot of quotes or proposals but you find yourself always the "runner up," it may be time to decide that you have better things to do than deal with such competition and decline to bid next time they call.

With customers and influencers fully discussed—and both are serious competition if you are often a single-source supplier—it's time to turn attention to "third party" or more external forms of competition, starting with the government.

Competition Checklist

Here are some questions to assist you in identifying the extent of influencer competition.

✔ Do you sell your services to larger organizations with multiple departments and several levels of management?

✔ Have you recently lost a long-time customer shortly after the contact/incumbent changed in the position you deal with?

✔ When your contact at a prospective customer is new to the position, is the previous incumbent still employed elsewhere at the organization?

✔ Does the person you deal with express enthusiasm for what you do but have difficulty obtaining approvals?

✔ Does your customer/client have formal committees to review all purchases?

✔ Is your customer/client organized along with the lines of what is known as a "matrix organization"?

✔ Do you prepare a lot of quotes or proposals for intermediate organizations (rather than end-users) or otherwise use referrals heavily to seek business?

✔ Does a new or prospective customer/client ask you to come in and present your services to several people rather than a single decision-maker?

Key Points to Remember

☞ Always expect the unexpected with influencers. There is not always a straight-line connection between a decision-maker you meet with and the influencers they listen to or receive input from. Since you cannot predict from company to company who the influencers are, independent investigation for each client firm is called for.

☞ Influencer behavior is more often biased and irrational than logical. The same factors that govern customer-origin competition (reluctance to change, bad past experiences, etc.) come into play.

☞ Competition originating with influencers can also be triggered very quickly; personnel changes or turf wars at the client's firm are two of the bigger triggers.

☞ External influencers, such as other consultants who are providers of non-competing services, need to be identified and their biases addressed.

☞ External influencers may also have relationships with one another; explore all joint venture, partnership, and subcontracting links.

CHAPTER 4

When Uncle Sam Is a Competitor

Although they claim they are "here to help you," if you are a service provider, when it comes to government (at all levels), this is far from the truth; you will often face a sizeable competitive threat from services provided by government departments and agencies. Governments are notorious for offering free services or, at best, cost-recovery services, all of which make it hard for for-profit enterprises in many sectors to compete. Such competition is doubly aggravating because it is your own tax dollars that go to fund it.

Undercutting the Private Sector

The way government activities can effectively squelch demand for private-sector services is illustrated in the following story. Several years ago, the U.S. Consulate General in Toronto approached a Canadian market research firm to conduct studies about the Canadian market for two U.S. companies interested in expanding north of the border. One of these studies was to focus on the jewelry findings sector, those companies supplying clasps, fittings for gemstones, and similar supplies, while another was to study demand for on-road, off-road vehicles. When the consultants saw the specs for the project, they were amazed. Incredibly detailed lists of questions indicated that the government expected a hefty report as an output. This was later confirmed in a phone conversation with the staffer at the Consulate responsible for the studies.

In the dollars of those days, the fees that should have been charged for each of these reports was in the range of $20,000 U.S. And what was the government prepared to pay? Approximately $1,000 U.S. per study, which was charged back to the requesting party. The Consulate felt this was quite reasonable for the amount of work involved, although in reality it would have required the market research firm to work below cost. Take this story out to its broader implications and it becomes obvious: Why would any company intent on exporting overseas directly pay a market research firm the $20,000 per study when it can get the answers it needs from the government at such a deep discount?

In this case, the U.S. Federal Government was brokering the work on a cost-recovery basis, but sometimes Federal departments—and not just in the United States—go one step further and prepare market studies and then distribute them to would-be exporters for free. The Canadian federal government's Department of Foreign Affairs and International Trade did so for many years. On analysis, these studies are very general, tend to rely exclusively on secondary information that has not been verified, and do not provide the depth of detail which a private-sector enterprise really should have before deciding to expand, particularly in a foreign country. But the temptation of acquiring something for free is usually too great and so many companies will rely just on this government source of information simply because the "price" is right.

Siphoning Off Opportunities

The U.S. Federal Government also provides well-organized and consistently low-cost competition to the private sector through the entity formerly known as Federal Prison Industries and recently rebaptized UNICOR. While the bulk of UNICOR's offerings include manufacturing or product-based activities, the organization is also a provider of services. And just which services does UNICOR offer? Signage, distribution and warehousing, printing and data services, lab services, and remanufacturing of equipment are just some. Nor is there a lack of sophistication in these offerings.

UNICOR's data services comprise geographic information systems (GIS) and computer-assisted design (CAD) applications, work on patents, technical manuals and bathymetric charts, electronic distribution, and forms of document conversion. In the area of environmental services, the laboratory offers electrical and environmental tests, including climactic simulation, performance evaluation of electronic cables and specialized contract assemblies. All work is performed to industry standards, such as military standards specs. An extensive array of equipment, salt-fog chambers, high temperature ovens, hydrostatic vessels and more is available to perform these services.[1]

While finding some sort of work for inmates to perform is undoubtedly a valuable part of the rehabilitation process and no one will question the wisdom of discharged prisoners having skills with which to earn a living, it is debatable whether government should be providing products and services, at low cost, in marketplaces served by for-profit entities, when the funding for UNICOR may have come from the taxpayers themselves, many of whom own their own businesses. To be sure, UNICOR does a lot of its work for other government departments or related federal agencies. But it still represents a subsidized form of competition, notably to many small service businesses that might want to bid on those same government contracts.

Similar activities initiated by the Canadian government also provide a "thorn in the flesh" for services entrepreneurs in Canada. There, the organization is CORCAN and telemarketing services are one of the offerings. While the objectives of CORCAN are noble—provide work and training for inmates at medium- and minimum-security facilities—the price competition is not. Earning levels for the inmates at one call center run in conjunction with CORCAN are $1.50 to $2.50 CDN per hour, significantly lower than statutory minimum wages or rates telemarketing companies in large centers have to pay, which are around $9 to $10 CDN per hour.[2]

Such practices have not escaped the attention of business advocates in either country. In the United States, the National Federation of Independent Business[3] has backed bills presented to Congress to curb the practice, while in Canada, the Telecommunications Workers Union has spoken out against the practice. But for anyone operating a for-profit service business that competes against such enterprises, this represents a form of competition that businesses could live without.

More Than the Federal Government

Government at levels below the federal also provide competition in services to private-sector enterprises. There was a time, for example, when municipal governments restricted their activities to providing water and sewage services, garbage collection, street maintenance, including snow removal and similar basics. Nowadays, in large urban areas, municipal or city governments frequently get involved in services as diverse as theater management, job counseling for welfare recipients, property management, organizing art exhibits, and the like. Many of these services are based on professional expertise and it is a matter of some debate whether government should really be in these businesses, since again, it is business owners' tax dollars that are funding many of these activities.

The same potential lurks at the state level in the U.S. as well. From the smaller states, like Rhode Island, on up to the most populous, like California, the tentacles of government reach far and wide. A quick perusal of Rhode Island's services shows a multitude of free services for business (which would have to be obtained for a fee elsewhere) such as financing advice, staff development and market development, and offerings in water testing, employment services, nutrition counseling and more, all of which have for-profit counterparts.[4]

Even more diverse services corresponding to those available from the private sector, are found during a scan of California's offering. Laboratory services, veterinary services, business services (including promotion, development, and market research), GIS data services, fairs and expositions, economic research, employment services, exporter services and marketing services are just some available.[5] While it is true that certain customers for state services—such as those aimed at children and teens—would not be in a position to acquire them on a market basis, there is a strong suggestion that the presence of "free" services from government does siphon off a certain market share from for-profit enterprises.

And in other developed or industrialized nations, the same story occurs. For-profit enterprises pay taxes, which often go to fund government initiatives that compete directly against the firms working to come up with the taxes!

Hidden Competition

The breadth and depth of government services may be hidden and can act as a competitive factor, without detection, for many years. This was the situation faced by People Inc., an organization based in western New York, which wanted to expand its training and support offerings to the disabled. People Inc. wanted to introduce a school-to-work transition program for those it described as "developmentally disabled."

Prior to launching its own school-to-work program, People Inc. decided to find out just what else was being offered. What emerged from their investigation was a wide array of programs, often "hidden" within broader school-to-work programs that catered to students of all ability levels. Furthermore, many of these government-sponsored programs (offered via colleges or schools) were at low cost or had their funding "taken care of" in some way. To this factor had to be added the competition of customer and influencer behavior, as many in the position to refer students to programs made reflexive choices, and went with the "usual suspects," rather than looking to the broader marketplace.

A Question of Favoritism?

Even if not competing directly against service businesses, government may find ways to engineer indirect competition. Such interference in the marketplace not only represents a hidden form of competition but also can amount to favoritism. This was the situation facing an environmental services company in dealing with the Ontario Ministry of the Environment a few years ago. This firm offered an approach to hazardous waste management, which involved newer technologies and produced better results at lower costs than older, competing technologies. Every time the firm tried to get in to see key officials at the Ministry (the firm needed to be on an approved list to roll out their marketing campaign), they were stonewalled. Given the mandate of government departments to manage the public purse effectively, this was surprising. Then the environmental service firm heard rumors of a letter, supposedly originating with the Ministry, which urged consulting engineering firms to spec the services of one of their competitors, which marketed an older technology. Concerned that such initiatives by a government ministry represented unfair interference in private sector competition, the firm set out to do some intelligence gathering among the influencer group—the engineers—to see what it could learn and find ways to address the "roadblocks" they faced in marketing their service. Had they not taken such steps, they would have indefinitely faced a formidable competitive threat in a key market.

Even when governments do not play favorites, they can also influence or stimulate competition via other interference in the marketplace. Subsidies or low-cost loans to business start-ups are a frequent tool to this end; particularly in areas of high unemployment or during recessions, governments will dabble rather heavily in the private sector by fostering the development of various service businesses.

Such subsidies or loans can be galling to the other operators of a range of businesses: word processing services, personal care services, printing, distribution, and other sectors become vulnerable. Only those services sectors where a professional designation is mandatory seem to be immune to this competitive factor. What is particularly irritating is that the established service firm, which has been getting by without such subsidies or low-cost loans and may be facing difficulty in obtaining or keeping its financing, especially during a recession, must now compete against a firm with little or no track record but a sizeable "pot" of funding to tide them over while they build up their business.

Crossing Borders

Not recognizing government in other countries might be a competitive factor, where government at home is not, can trip up a service business intent on expanding outside its home markets. A company operating call centers nationwide in the United States decided they wanted to increase their presence in the Canadian marketplace. They already had experience providing support to health insurers in the United States and decided that rolling out, based on this expertise in the Canadian marketplace, made sense. As they were less familiar with Canada, they decided to first commission some market research to determine where the best prospects were and learn who they should approach to pitch their services. An overview of current competition was another objective. A company was therefore engaged to undertake a study.

The call center company had assumed that hospitals would be one group to be targeted, while clinics providing outpatient services and those offering rehabilitation services for accident victims would be another segment. The company was also interested in learning about opportunities in the "hotline" segment of the market, where consumers who had health care or medical questions could call in for very basic information, e.g., what to do if a child has a fever, what to do if someone has had a fall, etc.

When the research came back, the call center company found itself with a very confusing array of choices. The hospital segment had recently been restructured along regional lines and each of the ten provinces had a different bureaucratic structure. Some provinces had restructured in name only whereas others had gone a step further and set up physical organizations to manage the hospitals. When it came to the clinics serving outpatients, some were publicly funded and some were privately operated. As for the hotline segment of the market, several hotlines existed, backed by an abundant supply of free information available to the public. Overall, there were few central decision-makers for any of the segments anywhere in the country.

Furthermore, where decision-makers had been reached, few had expressed an interest in call center support. Decision-makers at the hospitals could not understand why they would need call center support while the private clinics claimed they had no need to field calls 24 hours a day. Similar responses were given for the other segments targeted. What the call center company came to realize was that other call center operators were not the primary competition in the Canadian market but that the presence of government, its structure and mandates, was. As other call centers faced similar obstacles in the health care sector, they were secondary competitors at best; making any headway in Canada for the firm intent on expanding would rest on finding ways to best government either as a direct source of competition or as a major influencer of buyer or user behavior.

Indirect Competition

Setting up shop to compete with for-profit entities or playing favorites are not the only ways governments become a form of competition. Competition is created by legislators and regulators when they interfere in the workings of the marketplace, either by the legislation they do—or don't—pass or by the regulatory initiatives they introduce, such as deregulation of an industry.

A change to the legislation altered the playing field for many telecommunications companies in both the U.S. and Canada, as the challenges facing one player, Call-Net, show. The government, by changing the legislative climate in Canada, opened the way to "an all-out war among the traditional phone companies, the cable-TV industry and a growing band of feisty upstarts such as MetroNet Communications Corporation of Calgary and Call-Net Local Services Group Incorporated of Toronto, an affiliate of long-distance provider Sprint Canada Inc."[6] In such an environment, competitive factors shift rapidly, with today's competitors often becoming tomorrow's partners or even acquisition targets. This occurred when Call-Net acquired fONOROLA.[7] However, none of the subsequent competition or the need to monitor new types of competitor would have occurred without actions at the government level. Here the government was the indirect form of competition, with traditional and not-so-traditional competitors merely bit players on the stage. Similar developments were also seen in Europe in 1998 when markets for telecom services businesses were deregulated there. Over the long-term, further competition in telecom services, spurred on, in part, by government initiatives, will likely see a blending of lines between long-distance services, local services, mobile/cell telephony, online, video/broadcast, and possibly satellite services.

A continent-wide form of competition was also introduced, perhaps unwittingly, by the U.S. and Canadian governments when they signed the North American Free Trade Agreement (NAFTA) into effect. Several industry sectors were affected by NAFTA, some positively, some negatively, but the experience of the Canadian Standards Association (CSA) does show how a once-thriving enterprise can see its business decline due to legislative change. Although CSA had long faced some competition, notably from groups like Underwriters Lab (UL), the presence of the Canada-U.S. border had created a protected turf; there were requirements for certain products to be certified by CSA for the Canadian market, even if they had already received UL approval in the U.S. Under NAFTA, this requirement no longer held, and a UL or similar certification was good enough for both markets. Companies making the products that historically required CSA's services were not about to pay twice for the same service, and so demand for the organization's services dropped—by half. This left CSA looking south of the border to find ways to become the "certifier of choice" in direct competition to UL and other testing/standards agencies. But these direct or traditional competitors weren't the primary source of competition; the introduction of NAFTA, by the government, was.

Then, there are times when this indirect competition from government actions precipitates disastrous consequences, as can be seen in the electricity services market in California where, by 2001, the deregulated environment had led to supply and capacity problems, soaring costs, and power blackouts. Leaving aside problems at the industry level, each power provider faced a set of new issues. External competition had not really existed before; now independently owned utilities (IOUs) faced it on two fronts: customers who could defect to other suppliers and a range of other providers, such as other IOUs, Munis/Coops, and Marketers.[8] Then there were internal competitive factors to reckon with, such as a lack of skills to take new approaches with marketing, branding, and business diversification. The government's act in deregulating unleashed a Pandora's box of competitive forces.

Is it any wonder, when such experiences have affected some services sectors, that the practitioners in other sectors work so diligently to stave off any government interference? It is not without reason that many professional services—whether medical, legal, management consulting, or others—opt for self-regulation rather than risk having government calling the shots and creating undesirable competitive factors. If you operate a service business in a sector the government may be eyeing, both individual and collective vigilance is necessary to keep this form of competition at bay.

Tackling Uncle Sam as a Competitor

Luckily for any service firm concerned about competition emanating from government, most of what occurs in the legislative, regulatory, or administrative sectors of government is fairly transparent—at least in the developed or democratic countries. There are Web sites that allow you to see what government is up to, publications put out by government and independent coverage in the media. Plugging into these sources and networking at professional groups you belong to should keep you in the know.

Government competition may be an irritant—not quite what is meant by the government catchphrase "your tax dollars at work"—but it is not the only form of external competition to keep an eye on. There are also the other providers of the same or similar services among which lurk your traditional competitors and it is to these that we next turn our attention.

References

1. UNICOR Online: www.unicor.gov/schedule/index.ltm
2. "Call Centre in Prison Has Union Crying Foul." *Globe & Mail*. March 2, 2001: A1, A6.
3. "Prison Industry Poses Unfair Competition." *My Business*. September-October 2000: 23.
4. Rhode Island State Publications Clearinghouse: www.info.state.ri.us/azlist.htm
5. My California State Portal: www.ca.gov/state/portal/myca
6. "Open Season: The CRTC Clears The Way for War in the Phone Business." *Maclean's*. May 12, 1997.
7. "Call-Net Enterprises Inc. Challenges and Opportunities in a Continually Changing Environment" Ivey Management Services. 1998: 17.
8. "CI in a Newly Competitive Marketplace: A Case Study of the Electric Utility Industry." 13th Annual SCIP Conference Proceedings. March 25-28, 1998: 149-158.

Competition Checklist

Run through the following questions to help pinpoint the competition you face from government sources.

✔ Do you offer services for which the government also offers services through a group like UNICOR/CORCAN?

✔ When bidding on government contracts, do you frequently lose out to a lower bidder?

✔ Does the government have a mandate, such as in supporting exporters, which can lead to the availability of "for-free" services?

✔ Is the government in the position, via its role administering registration or certification processes, to play favorites?

✔ If you are selling your services outside your own jurisdiction, whether domestically or overseas, might you encounter different roles for government in your target markets than you face at home?

✔ Is the government in your market planning changes in legislation or regulation of markets?

✔ Is the government planning or threatening to take over regulation of your profession or industry?

Key Points to Remember

☛ Governments at all levels can transform themselves into competition by directly entering markets served by for-profit enterprises. In such cases, government-backed entities compete head-on by bidding directly on jobs for which private companies are also submitting bids.

☛ Other direct competition from government comes from services perceived as "free" by taxpayers (although most are paid for by individual taxes). Such government services fall into the category of alternates, as discussed in Chapter 2 under customer-origin competition.

☛ Subsidies and low-cost loans are another favorite form of indirect competition from the government. This form especially rears its head during recessions or during the summers, when students who cannot find jobs are encouraged to start their own businesses instead.

- Governments also set the stage for indirect competition by changes to legislation and regulations.

- Whenever a service needs to be registered or approved by government, the potential exists for the government to create competition by playing favorites.

CHAPTER 5

Traditional Competitors

Almost last of the external forces of competition, but certainly not least, comes what can be termed "traditional competitors": companies *purporting* to offer the same or similar services to your company, and which do represent a competitive threat but not in the same ways traditional competitors provide a threat in goods-producing industries. Another way to describe these competitors, given the many other sources of competition faced by a service business—and it is an important distinction—is as providers.

Providers Versus Competitors

While all the traditional competitors a service firm faces are providers, not all providers are competitors. The very realities of the services sector, as identified by Michael Porter and other writers—the fragmentation of each sector, the number of firms, their size and lack of clout—mean that many providers of, for example, recruitment services or public relations, separated by geography or target markets, may never actually compete with one another. One of the first questions to ask, especially if you are frequently a sole source (or single-source) supplier, is: Do you actually face competition from traditional competitors? There may be many client relationships where you do not; in such cases, it is customer or influencer competition you need to be most concerned about.

Assuming you do face traditional competitors—and these will be discussed in detail in Part 2—to arrive at the companies from among the universe of providers that merit your ongoing attention, you will need to consider which companies meet any or all of the following criteria:

- Firms that offer services fairly close to or the same as yours

- Firms that say they do

- Firms that offer viable alternatives (think back to the issues about alternates and substitutes raised in Chapter 2 to identify which players these might be)

- Firms that operate in the same markets as you

- Firms that serve the same customers as you do

The next point of examination is the degree of overlap between firms. Although other providers serve your customers or operate in your geographic territory, the extent to which their services overlap with yours and turn these companies into direct, traditional competitors on all fronts may be limited. One of the reasons traditional competitors in services do not invite an easy apples-to-apples comparison is that what is offered, within any given services sector, can vary quite greatly. Within the sphere of legal services, it is quite possible, for example, for lawyers who practice Marine Law to offer dissimilar services to their clients while still operating within the parameters of their legal specialty. Likewise, within the market research sector, there are many different methods that can be employed to investigate, for example, customer interest in a new product, customer satisfaction with an existing product, the response to a new brand or logo, etc. Research companies may employ telephone surveys, focus groups, mall intercepts, or other methodologies to probe these issues. The answers may be equally valuable to the client, but the means by which they are obtained will differ significantly.

This means any comparisons between your own company and those firms you might designate your traditional competitors will more usually fall into the arena of an apples-to-oranges comparison or possibly even apples-to-kumquats. This last comparison is particularly true when firms within a sector vary significantly in size; the resources and deliverables of one of the Big Five management consulting firms may be quite different from what is offered by a boutique firm and/or a sole practitioner. Yet, they are all likely to be compared one to the other by the clients, customers, or influencers when a purchase decision is being made. These disparities are yet one more of the variables that complicates the study and analysis of competition in the services sector.

Full or Partial Competitors

Once you have determined which firms seem to be traditional competitors, the next step is to consider how much competition they present to you. Some of the firms in this category may only need to appear on your radar screen when you are offering your services to certain sectors; for example, within the consulting engineering field, not all construction or capital projects firms build bridges. So two companies that always find themselves competing on highway contracts may not face each other across the bidding table if a bridge is up for tender. Such traditional competitors can be termed partial competitors; when the service offerings of such firms are placed on paper, such as in a Venn diagram, the amount of overlap between firms will cover only a quarter or a third of the other's business.

This is not true for those traditional competitors that might be termed full competitors; these are the firms that do seem to offer exactly the same services as yours and against whom you always go head-to-head with your clients.

While sifting through traditional competitors to see which match your firm across the board and those that only compete with you in some markets, it's important to remember that the best examination of your direct competition occurs from a "customer's eye view" of the market. This means that your field of competition changes, in all likelihood, from client to client. For Customer A, your competition may comprise Competitors One, Two, or Three; for Client B, the competitors may be Two, Four, and Six, and so on. This is why looking at both Full and Partial Competitors is so important. For your eventual CI gathering to pay off, you will want to be able to use it to win business *away from* these competitors. Without identifying your competition for each client, prospective customer, or lost account, you will not know the correct companies to study.

Issues of Visibility

Even as a list of full or partial competitors is being compiled, it is important to remember that most traditional competitors in services are *not* high profile. As will be explored in Chapter 8, just identifying where the industry begins and ends and spotting competitors that are low profile or downright hidden takes time. While some firms in a sector will be high profile, it is completely possible in many services sectors that one or more of the "powerhouses" are next to invisible.

In sectors such as investment advisory, legal advisory, or specialty fields such as knowing how to cap wildcat oil wells or refloat petroleum tankers, the individual with the most revered expertise may work from home, never advertise, and rely strictly on word-of-mouth marketing, an issue that will be examined in Chapter 11.

Imitators Versus Competitors

Since tackling the study of services competition is a rather overwhelming task, there are further ways to rank competitors so to allocate appropriate amounts of attention. Another type of provider that will occasionally come into view is the firm that might best be described as an imitator, rather than a competitor. In every services sector there are always firms that are the innovators and others that simply copy what the leaders are doing; this latter group is more appropriately termed an "imitator," not a competitor. Not only do imitators not innovate, they also may operate in what might be called a "parallel universe"; if your firm serves the blue chip, Fortune 500 customers and they only manage to land business with second-tier firms or regional players, they may also not represent head-to-head competition but instead be imitators. Another way this dichotomy manifests is in *who* you serve at the customer or client company. Even when both firms do serve the same companies, if your firm deals with only those in the executive suite or at the board level, firms that work strictly with middle managers—even if their service offering is similar to yours—may be less of a competitor and more of an imitator.

Not that such imitators should be dismissed from competitive intelligence work. Just as you may want to protect your turf against encroachment from such imitators, they may be working equally diligently to transform themselves and move up in the world. Imitators can—and often do—emerge, chrysalis-like, to become full-fledged traditional competitors, and so need to be monitored. They may transform themselves via acquisitions, taking on new personnel, or upgrading their deliverables; Part 2 will discuss how to probe these issues in greater depth to apply to situations such as the imitator.

Absentees and Exclusivities

Another issue to be aware of when identifying and studying traditional competitors is the impact on competitive dynamics and customer/influencer perceptions when a provider elects not to compete. This may come about because one of your traditional competitors has signed an exclusive with one company in an industry and so cannot work with others in that sector. For example, a management consulting firm may work with only one client in the automotive sector while a law firm may be restricted to just one telecom industry client.

While this may sound as if this gives other companies a clear run of the field, these absentees may actually be making it harder for your firm to land business. Just as too much competition, as discussed in Chapter 2, can paralyze customers into indecision, too little can have the same effect. And, when the absent firm has positioned and marketed itself as the premier supplier of certain services—issues discussed in Chapters 9 and 11—this absence can further leave the customers feeling they do not want to settle for second best (translation: your firm or others), effectively removing their business from the table.

New Market Entrants

As much as a service firm might wish its competitors, once identified, to remain stable and predictable, this is not a likely scenario; what is more likely is that one day you will wake up to find you are facing brand new market entrants—unless, of course, you undertake rigorous CI to make sure you spot such trouble before it spots you.

Given the ease with which many service firms can be opened (work at home or shared office arrangements make this possible, not to mention generous government financing as discussed in Chapter 4) the level of company creation in services will always remain high. Some of these new market entrants will go on to become sizeable traditional competitors while others will not; the rate of new business dissolution is 95 percent of all new businesses close within the first five years of operation.

While this means these market entrants are not here to stay, they need to be monitored as much for what they don't do as what they *do* do in the time they are in business. As discussed in earlier chapters, inexperienced or inadequate practitioners can unwittingly be "bad apples" who spoil things for everyone else. Incorrect pricing, inferior deliverables, and weak ethics are just some of the issues an established player needs to be monitoring for such new entrants, as they make the transition to either a full-fledged traditional competitor or a closed chapter in your industry's history.

And, while it is less about current competition, the issue of new market entries raises the question of competitors you will face if you ever decide to enter as-yet-unserved markets for yourself. Although all providers are not traditional competitors, as discussed earlier in this chapter, knowing who the other providers are may be of value if you decide to expand beyond your current geographic markets. As with all aspects of studying competition, there is no such thing as useless information; today's "nice to know" data can quickly become tomorrow's "need to know."

When Foes Are Friends, Too

There is another aspect of traditional competition in service businesses that needs scrutiny, and that is in the area of alliances or consortia, which may not be permanent but which are formed from time to time. While it is highly unlikely to think of some goods producers, such as Coca-Cola or Pepsi, deciding to go into partnership to sell a new soft drink, such working arrangements between traditional competitors are much more common in services.

To go back to the consulting engineering example, the two firms that go head-to-head on highway projects may end up partners on a highway and bridge project, with the firm lacking the bridge expertise subcontracting with its erstwhile highways opponent that actually has the know-how to erect a bridge. Such partnerships or consortia become even more common when the scale of the project increases to a proportion beyond the resources of any one firm; this is true in management consulting, consulting engineering, telecom services, and other sectors, especially when a large piece of international work is up for grabs. Consortia between firms in different countries are also likely to be formed for such purposes.

There is nothing wrong with this practice but, from a competitive intelligence point of view, such relationships need to be approached with caution because the information shared in a partnership today may form the basis of intelligence to be used by one of the firms against its former allies tomorrow.

Elements of Traditional Competition

Because Part 2 of this book looks at traditional competitors in detail, only a brief discussion of the elements of such competition is given here. It is important for a service organization to understand how traditional competitors run their businesses, how they serve and interact with their clients, especially face-to-face, and what they deliver. As the managers of any service business will tell you, all of these represent thorny issues that can be quite difficult and time-consuming to probe, mainly because they involve a lot of invisible factors.

Then, how any given service business is run will differ quite strongly from how any other is run, even if they all operate in the same sector. For example, do all the service businesses in your sector have their own premises? Or do they utilize what's known as serviced offices and outsource their activities? There can be a great deal of differentiation, for example, within the market research community where some companies not only manage research projects for clients, but also have phone rooms and resources to handle the research in-house. In other cases, the research "firm" is really a small cadre of managers who then outsource to other research companies that have phone rooms. This can have a tremendous impact on costs of services and thus pricing, not to mention quality control issues. Similarly, some ad agencies, publishers, design firms, and the like may have a host of services housed in one central location; others outsource heavily to a fleet of freelancers.

Directly related to the issue of organizational set-up is that of the cost structures sustained by the other providers you compete against. Is their rent for space higher or lower than yours? What are their wage structures like? Have they found ways to maintain marketing momentum while lowering their sales expense? Learning more about a traditional competitor's costs can be pivotal in understanding their pricing and learning when you may or may not be able to compete against them effectively. Knowing with which clients or for which jobs you do or don't have a cost and thus price advantage will allow you to channel your own resources for greater effect.

Tackling Traditional Competitors

Since ways to investigate and study traditional competitors are discussed in-depth further on, only a few notes are offered here. One of the more important tasks, before gathering detail about traditional competitors, is to first define which companies you really do compete against. One of the biggest traps in CI work is spending time (and thus money) probing companies that are not true competitors. Many people elect to study the top three companies in their industry, often because they are easy to spot and therefore easier to target. Such exercises have a tendency to yield nice-to-know information, rather than need-to-know!

Another benefit of fully determining who your traditional competitors are, as opposed to who you wish they were, is that, as you cast a wide net, you will identify the other providers against whom you do *not* compete. The advantage of this is that you will create a list of possible networking sources, people you can discuss business issues with, tap for advice, or possibly refer business to (or receive referrals from). Among the providers you do not compete with, there will always be some for whom one of your traditional competitors is a mutual competitor; in such cases, these non-competing providers can be tapped for exchanges of intelligence. If a provider is not a traditional competitor, there is also less risk in talking to them about industry concerns or thorny customer problems.

Competition Checklist

Use these questions to focus on the extent to which you have traditional competitors among the providers in your market.

✔ Are you always on a bidders list of potential suppliers, even with established clients, rather than being asked in as a sole source supplier?

✔ Do you frequently lose out, after being on the short list, to another provider?

✔ Do your services and those of other providers sound very much alike?

✔ Are you paying for a fully serviced office when the other providers in your markets are not?

✔ Do you employ considerably more people than the other providers in your market?

✔ Do the other providers enjoy higher staff retention rates than you do?

✔ Do the other providers in your markets have recruitment practices that land them better staff than you can hire?

✔ Do the other providers sometimes get "down and dirty" in how they conduct their business?

✔ Do the other providers hold more client events—such as seminars, golf days, retreats, etc.—than you do?

✔ Do the other providers spend more on client entertainment than you do?

✔ Do the other providers refuse to bid on work with certain clients or customers?

Key Points to Remember

☛ Perception is everything. Even when you are certain you have traditional competitors pegged, you will only derive value from CI efforts if you find out who the customers and clients perceive as your competitors.

☛ Market dynamics and competitive forces can be affected as much by companies that don't compete as those who do. Traditional competitors who opt out of serving certain customers may intensify customer-origin competition as your organization becomes seen as an also-ran.

☛ Imitators, those traditional competitors who offer the same or similar services but who operate in a "parallel universe" (serving regional as opposed to national clients, or middle managers at firms where you serve executives), introduce an extra element of competition, especially around pricing and deliverables.

☛ Providers in other markets, while not traditional competitors today, offer the greatest threat of future competition should they decide to enter your markets.

☛ Traditional competitors have many avenues open to them for seizing the agenda in your industry. Some ways are introducing alternates, reducing pricing levels, or migrating markets away from what you do.

CHAPTER 6

An Inside Job

Having surveyed all the external competitive forces discussed so far, each service business must next ask itself, "what are we doing internally to sabotage ourselves and provide our own form of competition?" Internal competition is much more prevalent in service businesses than it is in goods-producing businesses and can take many forms, ranging from the way a service business is organized or structured, through to issues such as personality conflicts between principals or partners.

Location as a Competitive Disadvantage

In Chapter 2 there was an example of how location can create perceptual competition in the eyes of the customer; the factor of "location, location, location" can also create other competitive disadvantages.

The provision of intellectual capital is, in theory, not location dependent, especially in the era of networks, but this may not translate into advantage in reality and where a business is based may prove a limitation to growth. Location must therefore be considered as a competitive factor. Although a firm may not need to be anywhere near its client companies to perform services, the perception that the services provider is "too far away" may prove too great a barrier to overcome to landing some organizations as clients. Or, if the service firm is in an area poorly served by public transport, or by very few airlines, the higher cost of bringing the consultant in for meetings may create a barrier. A service firm located "off the beaten track" may also be seen as having access to inferior support services, which in turn creates another competitive factor inhibiting growth. As a first step in assessing inside competition, a firm needs to look at how its location may work for or against it and, if there is a detrimental effect, how this can be overcome.

Organizational Structure as Competitive Barrier

Organizational structure can also be a competitive barrier acting to prevent your growth. In the case of larger service organizations, this barrier can come from the existence of multiple branches or locations, or where there is other geographic or divisional organization as is the case at the Big Five management consulting and accounting firms. Rather than all these entities working hand-in-hand to serve the customer and presenting a united front to the world—which is the underlying concept—they may, in fact, unwittingly work against one another and develop a sense of territoriality. These situations occur when one branch or division is slow to cooperate with another and causes the partner branch or division to lose out on a piece of business. In such cases, the traditional competitors may have submitted a weaker proposal or have less qualified staff, but the internal saboteur of intra-division dynamics prevents the better company, which should have won the business, from actually doing so. The repercussions this internal competition has on service and customer satisfaction will be looked at in Chapter 13.

Similarly, if approvals to proceed with a piece of business must be given by one department to another, such as by the purchasing, accounting, or credit departments to the sales or customer service departments, then internal bottlenecks may provide a greater source of competition than any actions taken by an outside competitor.

Such intracompany dynamics may prove a competitive threat when there are pronounced rivalries sapping the collective initiative. If account executives at an ad agency are not speaking to, say, design or creative people, the hostility sooner or later will spill over into the outside world and send the customers or clients flocking to an alternate supplier.

Even when the staff at a service business want to cooperate with one another, the realities of differences in location may conspire to be counterproductive, in spite of everyone's best efforts. If such departments are in separate buildings or, even worse, separate cities, no amount of modern technology, network fibers, videoconferencing, or similar devices can overcome the competitive disadvantage this arrangement inherently holds. The problems embedded in this situation can range from the awkwardness of using faxes to send items back and forward, or the limitations of e-mail, or the need to have real signatures on pieces of paper for approval. It may be the case that the overall business would thrive more if departments and locations were consolidated into one spot.

A Matter of Culture

Another way service firms create competition from within stems from the firm's culture. This can be particularly prevalent in longer-established firms that date back to an era of "gentleman's agreements" and the handshake to seal the deal.

Law is one area where old line firms have not always adapted as quickly as they might to new realities. Assuming that clients will remain loyal can be a major underpinning to such a lack of adaptiveness; this is a case where an external competitive factor, such as customer-origin competition, intersects with the internal factor of culture. Law firms in the habit of billing clients with "no questions asked" about the dollars have been brought up short by clients who will now question every dime. The fact such clients may be "shopping" for a new law firm at any given point in time represents a reality unheard of a decade or more ago.

Service firms may also be vulnerable if their own culture is very high-minded and they do not take into account the lack of ethics on the part of others in the larger environment, notably traditional competitors. Such a development can catch a firm unawares, especially when the actions of a competitor make little sense. This was the case for a consultant providing marketing support services to the pharmaceutical industry. A traditional competitor, based in the U.S., had begun selling their services in Canada. What surprised the Canadian consultant was the aggressiveness of the competitor over a market that is much smaller in size than the U.S., plus the "negative selling" tactics being used. The competitor was generally letting it be known that the consultant's firm could neither produce a report nor write one! This was far from the truth; once the consultant learned about his competitor's lack of ethics, he was able to address the situation, in a professional manner, in newsletters and in direct dealings with clients.

At a broader level, even when firms are signatories to industry codes of ethics, it is a liability of culture, at some firms, to assume everyone plays by the rules. Finding out what your competitors are doing in how they run their business and serve their accounts will allow you to address any unsavory developments. On the other hand, if the customers or influencers like the tactics of those who are abandoning ethics, the convergence of external and internal competition can easily overwhelm the firm with the stronger ethics, even if it is morally in the right. Studying your own culture plus your firm's ethical position will allow you to assess when or how you are "shooting yourself in the foot" by adhering to practices that are out-of-date.

Such cultural factors can also create a form of inertia, where appropriate action is not taken to deal with the new realities. There may even be an unwillingness to adopt practices that are found distasteful. Or, the firm may believe its existing service offering has such merits, as proven by past demand, that no innovations are needed. Such reliance on past practices may be the major source of competition for such firms, rather than specific, external initiatives by traditional competitors to introduce something new.

The Impact of Client Interaction

"Self-competition" can also be created in the ways you do or don't allow the customers or clients to interact with you. In recent years, a particularly formidable competitive barrier has been erected at many organizations, both goods-producing and service businesses, in the form of their phone systems. The integration of computers and telephones has led to some very fancy menu-driven systems, which, while they are technologically feasible, do not always make sense from the external customer's point-of-view. Navigating these often labyrinthine menus has proven a considerable turnoff to many a customer who has then taken his or her business to an organization with a simpler phone system. Some of the problems probably hark back to the issue already discussed: how your organization is structured. But since the very nature of a service business is just that, service—meaning there is no product for which service is simply offered as a back-up—then the manner in which your clients or customers reach you can be make-or-break in terms of the continuing financial health of the organization.

Consider the case of a well-known financial service firm that offers travel services and charge-card facilities. Even as a "member"—which ads assure all and sundry "has its privileges"—contacting a human representative at this organization is frequently an event equivalent to scaling Mt. Everest. When a "member" dials up, they're asked for their card number, a 16-digit affair that has to be punched into the phone. The caller is then routed through a numerical maze until the appropriate extension is found—again, the customer has to do all the work here—at which point the membership number has to be punched in again! This firm never lets on how many customers become frustrated and decide they can do without "membership" and its "privileges" but, based on popular myth, more than one person has been heard to brag that they cut up their card from this particular organization. Since it costs three times as much money to land a new customer than it does to retain an existing customer, this service organization's approach to its customers is quite surprising. It is equally strange that they would want to compete against themselves in this fashion. At the very least, any service organization intent on staying in business should offer the option of pressing zero to reach a live operator at several points throughout its menu-driven option.

Another way service businesses can create a form of competition themselves is in what they say to the marketplace at large and what they actually do. If a firm states publicly that it never works with a company earning less than $1 billion a year—as the former Andersen Consulting, now Accenture, did—and then turns around and works with a company earning "only" $500 million, then this sends conflicting messages into the marketplace. Such lofty goals also prove counterproductive and represent a competitive force when the economy sours. Staking out a turf in this way, in public, can boomerang if all the firm's clients experience reduced revenues. Does this mean the service firm won't work for those client companies anymore? What about the much-vaunted relationship that's supposed to endure through thick and thin? Competing against your own pronouncements—or being forced to backtrack on them—is a form of competition no service firm needs.

Likewise, if a firm makes much publicly of always delivering by overnight courier and then mails results to a client, its traditional competitors need do no more than sit back and watch the repercussions.

The Threat of Adamancy

Another way competition is created by internal forces is when service businesses take a position of adamancy in how they deal with their suppliers. Very few organizations nowadays are entirely self-sufficient in terms of the goods and services they must acquire from outside and this is particularly the case with service businesses in many sectors. As well as their own staff, advertising agencies rely on a fleet of freelancers of varying sorts to assist them. The same is true of many areas of the publishing business. Executive search firms and management consultants may also use outside suppliers for printing, research, event organization, and many other tasks.

Since it is widely recognized that you get what you pay for, you would think it would be a given that service businesses with any thoughts of longevity would automatically want to obtain the best help. This is not always the case and it is often not for the reason most would suspect—price—but rather a lot of rules that the business seeking the service sets up in how it deals with its outside suppliers. There may be rules about payment and when invoices are to be submitted, rather than trying to work with each supplier individually to develop a program of mutual benefit. There will also be issues in terms of deliverables, in that many organizations insist that the work the supplier has done be submitted only in a certain software or only in a certain format, regardless of how suitable or otherwise the software might be for the deliverable in question. In such cases, the supplier's possession of a piece of technology takes precedence over the excellence of the core service being purchased.

This was the situation faced by a supplier of competitive intelligence services that had received a Request For Proposal (RFP) from the telecom services company, Northern Telecom (Nortel), an organization operating globally. This telecom company exhibited strong adamancy in how it approached the whole subject and likely did not end up with the best services available in the marketplace. First, Nortel was adamant in that it made no attempt, prior to developing the specs, to contact any CI consultants and get their input on how the bid should be structured, what should be included, or to learn how other companies were approaching such RFPs. Then, the bid specs were released allowing a very narrow timeframe for response. They were sent out by courier on a Wednesday, delivered on a Thursday, with the proposals due the next day, on the Friday. This left most consulting companies with a window of 24 hours or less to put together their responses. Already, one suspects that Nortel had already eliminated the best suppliers through its adamancy.

This practice continued in that Nortel was demanding the deliverables be presented within the scope of a spreadsheet program, which they had decided would be structured into 120 cells. The assignment was to target 10 competitors and, for each competitor, investigate 12 services or products. The only problem is, the information that would be obtained during the CI gathering process might not fit so neatly and conveniently into those 120 cells, a frequent occurrence with CI or similar research work. There was also a presumption that the information would be obtained in 120 discrete pieces. Given that competitive intelligence draws on multiple sources and uses tools such as the in-depth interview, where a number of questions can be answered and several pieces of information obtained in one phone call, the structure for pricing the bid and providing the deliverables was completely divorced from how the information would be gathered. It is rather suspected that the only consultants who would respond to such a bid would be novices; more experienced consultants, with an established clientele, would ignore the situation or decline to respond to the RFP. This meant Nortel was really putting itself at a disadvantage with respect to its own telecom competitors. If other telecom service companies are more flexible in how they contract for CI—or any other services—they are more likely to end up with the best supplier.

Competing Against Staff Departures

One of the more common ways in which internal competition is fostered and provides a greater threat than external forces is in the way companies allow key employees to leave or do not otherwise address significant employee turnover within their own ranks. In most service organizations the people *are* the business and their expertise is what the customers are buying; not tackling this problem will have double the impact that turnover might in a goods-producing organization. This was the situation faced by the publisher of a number of trade magazines for associations and industry groups, which failed to closely examine the higher-than-average turnover amongst its sales representatives. As reps left the company, they were followed by the customers, who made their own decisions to place their business with the magazines where the reps they liked were now employed. This defection of key customers meant a steady trickle of advertising revenues away from the publisher. Before too long, the organization was in serious financial difficulty and had to discontinue several of its publications.

Customer defections will also follow if inside sales reps or customer service people leave and destroy the continuity that the customers expect when they phone up to do business. Similarly, in law firms, where specialized expertise may be what the customers are buying, should a lawyer leave to join another firm or go out on his or her own, it's almost a given that the customers will follow to where the expertise is. The importance of staff retention will be revisited in Chapter 15.

Creating Competition with Too Much Change

Disgruntled employees—and a major internal competitive factor—can arise if the organization adopts change at too rapid a pace. This has become particularly common with the advent of new technologies around the computer. No sooner do the staff learn one particular piece of software, than it's upgraded or replaced and everyone goes back to square one on the learning curve. The same can be true of hardware; no sooner do the technicians iron out the kinks in one system, than it's replaced with the latest must-have technology. Expecting employees to not only get their regular duties done, but to continually learn new equipment, new software and other new tools, makes the workplace doubly stressful and if it does not lead to employee attrition, it certainly leads to an intense inertia in the company as less and less real work is accomplished. One of the illusions of technology is that, by adopting the latest, you're keeping out in front; whereas, in reality, the company may be falling further and further behind relative to its traditional competitors. If competitors have decided to "sit tight" with what they have and devote their resources to customer service, then theirs will be the competitive advantage.

Even when a service firm does manage to retain all the key employees, results may be further handicapped if such personnel are not given the right resources or any resources at all. Expecting them to serve the customers or clients effectively under such circumstances and retain these for your business, and thus your revenues, is also unreasonable. Consider the future impact such self-sabotage will have on a company in the aeronautics industry, which decided to no longer subscribe to any print publications for its library. Someone, somewhere in the organization, had decided the company was to rely strictly on Web- and Internet-based information. All subscriptions to print journals, newsletters, newspapers, and trade magazines—which staff at this firm needed to keep up-to-date—were summarily canceled. Too bad, if the critical information this company needs is not available on the Web (as much isn't, particularly in the technical area); online sources are now the only ones that the staff of this company is allowed to use, on company time.

Curtailing resources in this way is often not seen as a competitive factor because the impact is not always immediately felt. Cutting out critical information sources will likely not show any adverse effect for the first six months to one year, but beyond this point the impact will be strong. This was true at a financial services organization where, one day, the number crunchers got the better of the in-house library and closed it down. Staff were laid off and materials were either sold or destroyed. As time wore on, the folly of this decision began to show itself. The staff responsible for preparing bids to land contracts for the management of large investments, such as pension funds, were less well-informed than their competitors and so the organization started to win fewer bids. This did not mean that the other providers or traditional competitors were better organizations but rather, in a comparative situation, they just seemed better informed, likely because they had not made such drastic reductions to their resource support. A further spinoff of this decision to axe the library was that new product development at the financial services organization began to take a beating and so other companies soon became seen as the gold standard in the business. By the time the organization realized it had made a mistake in paring resources so closely, the re-startup costs for the in-house information center were considerable and amounted to more in the first year they were restored than running the library had cost for the last three years of its operation.

Competition from Internal Saboteurs

The other ways service businesses can provide competition to themselves is when the staff they have hired, in spite of being admirably qualified for the tasks at hand, choose not to work very hard. These employees might be termed "fifth columns" and while they do not formally work for anyone else, they manage to work against your business and its goals. They also tend to undermine the efforts of other employees and damp down morale. Since such fifth column employees place a real brake on the growth of the organization, they are every bit as much a competitor as any external rival, who might be openly trying to siphon off your markets and customers.

These are the employees who work to rule, even though they aren't in a union, and never do any more than they have to. It can often include people who are described as not good enough to promote but not bad enough to fire. It can include employees who have been passed over for promotions and resent the fact. It can include employees who never quite achieved what they thought they should and have developed jealousy and animosity toward the firm's founders or leaders as a result.

Taken to an extreme, there are cases where employees become deliberate saboteurs, by linking up with a competitive firm to their employer. This was the experience at one market research company, which had been thriving. While the firm continued to bid on as many projects as before, its percentage of business landed from proposals submitted dropped to zero. An investigation eventually revealed that one of the company's receptionists had been feeding copies of proposals to a competing firm, in return for a finder's fee for any business this other firm landed. While an employee in a goods-producing business who is stealing may quickly be spotted, it is a lot harder to detect the machinations of an employee up to such activities in a service firm, because the "theft" is harder to spot. All the receptionist had to do was make an extra set of photocopies of the proposals, which were still sent to the prospective clients. The competitor then followed up and put in a lower bid and otherwise undermined the original firm; in a recession, which was then on, the clients did not resist the temptation of reduced fees. Although the company's principal followed up with the clients about the proposals, they never called back—or so it seemed. It was only later that the firm's management realized the receptionist was deliberately not passing on the messages when such calls were returned.

Clashes of Ego

Professional services firms also harbor another form of competition in the personalities of their partners or principals. Such firms are often "rife with contentiousness and self-interest, the building of fiefdoms, insensitivity to clients, exploitation of staff professionals and slow and inefficient decision-making."[1] This was certainly true at Lasik Vision Centers, where the internal warfare between the founder-surgeon and the CEO served to create an internal source of competition, which not only hurt Lasik Vision but had a detrimental effect on the entire industry.

With Lasik Vision, an organization that grew from one location to thirty-one in less than three years, differences of opinion about the wisdom of rapid growth and pushing up the number of procedures performed, not to mention the spiraling down of the price charged, per eye, for vision correction, led to the firing of the CEO by the founder-surgeon and a spate of lawsuits. While such in-fighting was sapping Lasik Vision internally, the price reductions also forced other operators of laser vision correction centers into reactive mode; they were forced to either lower their prices or find ways to differentiate what they did continent-wide in North America. The refractive surgery industry, as late as 2001, was still suffering from losses and declining share prices because of an internal personality conflict originating at just one of the industry's key players, a conflict that can be traced back to 1998.[2]

How other industry players might have been better able to deal with the spillover effect of this source of competition—and how Lasik Vision itself might have been able to contain it—will be discussed in some of the chapters in Part 2 of this book.

Tackling Inside Competition

While it may seem easy to track inside competition, very often service business operators do not notice right away what is happening right under their noses. Or, they may decide internal issues are so obvious that they don't require any special effort.

Before any service firm operator decides to ignore this issue, he should remind himself of this fact: "The traditional competitors are studying us to spot our weaknesses no less than we are studying them." Any form of internal competition discussed in this chapter, if left unchecked, will deliver a superb advantage to other providers in your industry, especially when they find out about it and you don't.

So much competition, so little time to study it all. Any service business can be forgiven for thinking this, but, wait, there's still more. Before examining in Part 2 how to study traditional competitors in-depth, consideration needs to be given to all the other forms of competition—left-field competition—which can rear up and make your life miserable.

References

1. "Managing Knowledge & Relationships: Sustaining Success in Professional Services." Darden School Working Paper. 1996: 26.
2. "Wrongful Dismissal, Corporate Foul Play, Medical Negligence." *R.O.B. Magazine.* January 2001: 36-40, 42, 44.

Competition Checklist

Find out the extent to which your firm provides inside (self-generated) competition using the following questions.

✔ Does the mere mention of where your service business is located dilute the interest of prospective customers?

✔ Does your firm have several offices, located in different geographic areas that are supposed to work together?

✔ Do the staff at your various locations often work against one another?

✔ Does your internal culture date from times past or assume conditions which no longer exist?

✔ Have you set up phone systems that are intended to save your firm money but require a lot of tedious effort from your customers/clients?

✔ Do your clients frequently question your bills or debate the value of the work they have received?

✔ Do you have one set of procedures for dealing with all your suppliers, no matter what type of deliverable they provide?

✔ Does some secondary element of the service being procured, such as requiring suppliers to use only one type of software, take precedence over the primary element or core competence of what is being bought?

✔ Have you been experiencing higher than normal turnover in your staff?

✔ Have you been introducing new technologies, new procedures or other changes at an overly rapid rate?

✔ Have there been arbitrary decisions made by the managers at your firm about discontinuing internal support services or no longer providing training and continuing education for staff?

✔ Have there been any nagging or suspicious changes in behavior among your staff, particularly long-service and supposedly loyal personnel?

✔ Do the partners and principals fight continually?

Key Points to Remember

☛ A strong competitive force is potentially generated in the ways your firm interacts with outside parties, whether customers/clients or suppliers. Analyze these interactions objectively to eliminate detrimental factors.

☛ Change for the sake of change is another way internal competition is created. Examine the merits of anything your company plans to introduce to see if the benefits really outweigh the disadvantages.

☛ Limiting internal resources also serves as an impediment and hands advantage to external traditional competitors, with no particular effort on their part. Make sure staff have the right tools to get the job done.

☛ Employees with contrary agendas are a potent weapon—in the favor of traditional competitors. Make sure all fifth columns are identified and dealt with appropriately. Especially take steps to eliminate any outright saboteurs.

☛ Partners and principals can often lose sight of the company's goals or get waylaid by personal agendas. This creates the most potent inside competition of all.

CHAPTER 7

Left-Field Competition

Keeping an eye on external and internal competition you know about or can predict, as discussed in the last six chapters, is not enough; operators of businesses in the services sector are not immune from the many other competitive factors that can arise out of nowhere, unexpected, unexplained, or unpredictable, and go on to cause disruption. Such competition can, of course, cause problems for the goods-producing sector as well, but the intensity of pain is often greater in services, primarily due to the key characteristics outlined in Chapter 1; services businesses are mainly smaller entities, owned by an individual or group of individuals, and are more vulnerable to a range of disruptive developments in the outside world.

The surprise element of such developments has led to the term "left-field competition." While it is not always possible to determine when and where this competition can arise, at least remaining alert to some of the factors that make up left-field competition means you will be caught less unawares. This can be an especially valuable awareness for newer businesses that lack the compass, born of experience, which guides more established firms.

Sudden Changes in Demand

One of these forms of left-field competition is rapid shifts in a marketplace or a population. A sudden increase in demand—which sounds like a positive development—may leave a smaller company, in particular, unable to keep up with the pressures or unable to maintain its usual quality and service levels. And, as the company falters, new traditional competitors may suddenly enter the marketplace to satisfy needs that are not being met. To focus only on these new market entrants is to miss the point of what really formed the competitive force: It is the good times that set the stage for other companies to seize opportunities.

Conversely, when a customer company in a smaller geographic center suddenly announces it is closing a facility, throwing several hundred employees out of work, the ripple effect—if this closing was quite unexpected—can hurt many small service businesses in the neighborhood from personal services firms through to those offering professional services, such as law and real estate. If the loss of employment opportunities at the customer company further lead to a mass exodus of residents from a given locale, the damage will be even more pronounced.

Financial Fluctuations

Another type of change that represents left-field competition for service businesses is a change in the interest rates charged by financial lenders, mainly when interest rates rise very steeply. Few companies of any longevity in services are not dependent on some form of credit, such as a revolving line; when interest rates soar, having deep pockets may be the determinant of whether a company can stay in business or not, rather than the quality of its services, until rates level out. This was the situation faced by many insurance companies when interest rates climbed steeply and people began borrowing against their policies at the much lower rates listed on those policies. Those insurers that could not cover the differences or ran into cash-flow problems as a result were placed in a difficult position and often ended up being acquired or bought out by better funded insurers.[1]

Wanting It All, Wanting It Now

The emergence of what is known as 24/7 service, around-the-clock support for services as varied as airline travel, merchandise ordering, insurance coverage, and banking, represents another form of left-field competition that could not always be predicted nor expected by those in the services sector. Even in conventional retailing, many smaller operators have been put at a disadvantage by larger firms that can operate around-the-clock. In such cases, large companies are in a position to set up distributed call centers and absorb the costs of their around-the-clock maintenance. The smaller service provider may not have the resources to compete. The impact of customers expectations for 24/7 service are discussed in Chapter 13, where an examination of service and customer satisfaction is made.

The Tentacles of Technology

The last 25 years of the 20th century witnessed an unprecedented surge in technological innovations, notably those based on the personal computer. While such technology has been a boon to many service firms, it has also introduced an unexpected competitive force into the marketplace.

One of the ways technology represents a concrete form of left-field competition is when a market entrant, coming in to a particular services sector and starting from scratch, is able to purchase or acquire state-of-the-art technology and put all other service providers in this sector at a disadvantage. This was true when FedEx decided to move beyond its core small package business into other delivery services; its state-of-the-art technology plus the company's logistics experience enabled it to ramp up fairly quickly and put existing competitors at delivery, turnaround, and pricing disadvantages. Such a scenario is particularly common after a recessionary period when existing service firms, the survivors who have survived either the high interest rates as discussed previously or a drop in demand for their services, are cash-strapped and cannot afford the level of investment necessary to fight back. Such competitive disadvantage is further aggravated if the new market entrants receive lavish government grants, sources of funds that are only available to new businesses, not the stalwarts who have been paying taxes through tough times.

While still looking at technology, it is impossible to overlook the emergence of a facility like the Internet and the Web, which has also presented a new form of competition for many service providers. Rather than technology always resulting in the export of business opportunities to a competing provider overseas, Internet/Web-based businesses can also siphon customer attention to service providers miles away from where the customer or client lives. Certainly, Internet/Web technologies allow the customers to consider a wider field of competition in meeting their needs. There are even cases where individuals may not have been customers for a particular type of service prior to a technology option becoming available. A service like Amazon.com, which essentially ships books to customers (although a product is part of the purchase, this delivery service is also part of what is being bought), caters to a certain segment of the population that had no prior or existing book purchase habits and would not visit a bookstore if Amazon.com did not exist.

Another irony of technology as a source of competition is the extent to which service providers operating solely within an electronic arena are now facing their own competition, sprung solely from within the technological domain in which they operate. Whereas companies like E*Trade Securities historically provided an electronic challenge to mainline "bricks-and-mortar" stockbrokers, E*Trade itself now faces new competition within the sphere of technology it once dominated. Companies like eBroker and Schwab represent rivals that have moved to beat E*Trade at its own game.[2]

Other services sectors, which only ever existed in a virtual domain, likewise find themselves challenged by newer permutations of technology. The older DIALOG and LexisNexis online database services, plus their newer brethren, AOL and CompuServe, now face competition for their customers from the Internet, the Web, telephone and cable companies, content companies, Internet Service Providers (ISPs), and browser/search engine companies.

This may allow any number of service firms to take heart; while keeping up with technology-driven competition may prove a headache for all except the wealthiest firms, there is a suggestion that the very progenitors of such competition may end up beaten at their own game!

Labor and Labor Costs

Left-field competition also appears in the guise of offshore labor or, more specifically, offshore labor rates. This competitive factor had a major impact on the software development industry when companies based in the United States started outsourcing development of software to programmers in places as far-flung as Russia and India. Just as the North American goods-producing sector had to face this form of competition when companies began to set up factories in lower cost countries in the Orient and the *maquiladora* belt of Mexico, providers of services now found themselves competing with a much more widely distributed array of competitors. While it is unquestionably technology that has enabled this development, technology alone is not the competitive factor in this case, as such networks obviously allow people, at least in theory, to outsource to *higher cost* locations as readily as lower cost. Technology is therefore something of a mirage when pieces of service business are shipped overseas and the real source of competition is the lower labor costs of the producer based offshore.

Another way labor—which is really the backbone of a service business—can cause havoc is when a work force decides to unionize. In a services environment, where "spinning on a dime" to serve the customers is often the determinant of continuing in business, such a development can sound the death knell for the company, especially a smaller firm. Although unionization may be perceived as the preserve of "blue-collar workers," this is not factually correct; in some countries, even doctors are in unions! No firm, whatever the service provided, can consider itself immune from such a development; unions have attempted to organize bank tellers, Walmart staff, fast-food workers, teaching assistants at universities, and others. In some cases, such unionization efforts have been successful, leaving the service firm with a new form of inside competition to deal with.

Per-Capita Competition

Labor also especially represents a competitive factor for service businesses during economic boom times. Unlike automated production lines, which can be speeded up to produce more, there is a finite element to human labor. There are a set number of adults of working age in the market for work; this fact, along with realistic restrictions on how many hours a day they can productively work, hamper service business growth—or even survival—when times improve so much that the unemployment rate drops. The fact that service companies may resort under these conditions to hiring any warm body they can find also represents a competitive factor of the inside competition variety discussed in Chapter 6; such hires may not really meet the demands of the business, contributing to an erosion of customer confidence, no less than a lack or absence of employees may drive the business down. Coupled with the problems discussed above, when there is an unexpected upswing in demand such developments can quickly sound the death knell for a service firm. As such, these developments are a potent form of competition.

Smaller service firms may also find themselves at a competitive disadvantage in boom times against the recruitment initiatives of larger firms—whether or not these firms represent traditional competitors—as the bigger organizations usually have deeper pockets and can offer more attractive packages to the steadily dwindling pool of qualified labor. Small distribution companies, design firms, placement agencies, and the like may find themselves competing with the Big Five management consulting firms while all services sector organizations may find themselves up against the recruitment initiatives of the goods-producing sector.

Rationalization as Competition

Another form of left-field competition is a trend, such as globalization, where certain companies, notably larger and internationally owned companies, start rationalizing their operations and shifting their business around. For many service companies, particularly smaller service companies that depend on larger organizations for much of their business and thus their cash-flow, this can have a dramatic and often devastating impact on the size of their business and the demand for their services. This was the outcome for many service providers (ad agencies, research companies, designers, public relations firms, and more) when the then-Marion Merrell Dow organization decided to close most of its operations in Canada. Although the pharmaceutical company had just moved into spanking new quarters, a corporate decision made overseas quickly mothballed everything, laid off most of the staff at MMD Canada, and wiped out client relationships of long standing for many smaller service firms.

Hidden Competition

Competition may also be buried within the bowels of an organization not in your industry sector at all, nor readily identifiable as a competitor. Such providers are not the traditional competitors already discussed in Chapter 5.

Rather, they are companies like ADP, which went beyond its traditional payroll handling activities to offer bank accounting and tax filings for its customers and their employees. Once this delivery was seamless, the company added ERISA reporting, personnel records, and financial analyses. As a final step, personalized communications, such as adding slogans, messages, or logos on checks, or including notes with employees' paychecks, were offered. In this way, ADP—still perceived by most as a payroll company—actually competes with those offering tax preparation services, HR and personnel consultants, financial planners, printing services, publishers of employee newsletters, and communications consultants.

Not recognizing competition that may, at best, be hidden or, at worst, unrealized or embryonic can capsize a service business, especially during the start-up phase. When Bank of Montreal set out to launch its virtual banking service, mBanx, it knew that vigilance over new or unexpressed forms of competition was essential to success. The regular or traditional competitors, which the bank dubbed direct competition, comprised the other banks in its markets in Canada, the U.S., and Mexico. The changing regulatory environment for financial services also meant other virtual banks—such as VanCity Savings and Trust's new Citizens Bank division—could provide competition, along with ventures launched by credit unions, insurance companies, and even Microsoft.

Associations can also provide hidden competition. Much like the government-as-competitor discussed in Chapter 4, associations, which take your money and promise to represent you and others in your industry, can then turn around and compete with you. There are several thousand associations in the U.S. alone, most supported by dues-paying members who seek collective representation for dealing with industry-wide concerns. Some ways this form of competition operates are discussed in Chapter 8.

This was the major form of competition that a commercial seminar company encountered when considering expansion into the U.S. market. The firm's major expertise rested on providing seminars in three categories: tax and securities, corporate finance, and intellectual property. Believing competition would come from other commercial seminar providers, the firm concentrated its investigations solely in this sphere. However, the results kept coming back the same: no such seminars were being offered by commercial providers. This didn't make sense; at the time, intellectual property was a hot topic due to the level of counterfeiting in industry sectors such as software, while NAFTA had opened a host of new issues in the area of tax and securities.

It was only when the seminar provider's investigation took a broader look at the marketplace that it found its competition. In the U.S., mandatory upgrading and continuing education requirements in the legal and accounting professions meant all such programs were offered under the aegis of professional associations. The "lock" of these groups on the market was enough to keep the commercial providers away.

Commoditization

A final form left-field competition can take is the trend to commoditization, which overtakes services. Since this process can happen slowly, it is often not detected until it is well entrenched. This has happened to services such as tax accounting and auditing, where customers for such services can switch from one supplier to another, with little impact on their businesses, at the end of a contract period. There is often too little to differentiate between suppliers and so, to the purchasers, it is all the same to them which accounting firm is used.

One of the tip-offs that this commoditization process is occurring comes when the decision to choose one professional services firm over another turns increasingly on price, not expertise or devoted service in the past; perceptions about the value of the expertise being purchased and the relative merits of the individual professionals at any given firm do not enter the equation. Finding ways to spot traditional competitors' tactics for dealing with commoditization are discussed in Chapter 9.

References

1. "Will Services Follow Manufacturing Into Decline?" *Harvard Business Review*. November-December 1986: 95-103.
2. "E*Trade Securities Inc." Stanford Graduate School of Business. July 1996: 15.

Competition Checklist

The following questions will assist you in identifying the left-field competition you face.

✔ Have you ever been overwhelmed by a sudden surge in demand?

✔ Have you ever lost any customers/clients during boom times?

✔ Have you ever experienced cash flow problems when interest rates change?

✔ Have your clients or customers told you they have switched suppliers to obtain around-the-clock support?

✔ Have you lost a customer or client to a service located more than 500 miles away from your location?

✔ Do you find the names of companies located in other countries on the bidders' list for work you compete for?

✔ Have your staff ever expressed collective dissatisfaction with working conditions, hours of work, or other variables?

✔ Have you ever had trouble recruiting staff?

✔ Has there been a lot of consolidation in your industry, with many mergers or acquisitions occurring?

✔ Have you ever lost out on a piece of business to an organization not in your industry or to one you have never previously heard of?

✔ Are clients or customers increasingly disinterested in any unique attributes you bring to the table?

✔ Are customers or clients increasingly making decisions solely on price?

Key Points to Remember

☞ Left-field competition often originates with broad trends, changes that can be termed mass movements. Commoditization of services, surges in demand, global reorganizations of business, all fall into the category of mass movements.

☞ Labor availability and costs are also the seeds of further left-field competition. Shortages, competition from dissimilar industries for scarce labor, the cost of labor in other geographic areas, are just some of the ways this manifests.

☞ Technology can form a major competitive threat, particularly in the way it changes rapidly. Even those businesses that exist solely because of technology are not immune to being undone by it.

☞ Another form of left-field competition is that which resides in organizations, just where you'd least expect. Private sector companies and associations are just two possibilities; even worse, they may offer competing services for free.

☞ Being a survivor of tough times creates another form of competition when newer, better-heeled entrants appear and enjoy an immediate advantage over the battle-scarred.

PART 2

THE

COMPETITIVE

ISSUES

CHAPTER 8

Where Are They?

Suggesting that a service business should study its competition assumes that the business knows where its competitors are. And one of the initial challenges facing any services firm intent on understanding competitive forces in the marketplace is that the competition may be low profile or hidden all together. Before you can study the competition, you first have to find it.

A further complicating factor, in identifying and understanding your traditional competitors, comes from the nature of service businesses. Those entities offering services that may fall into the same bailiwick as yours can include sole practitioners, people working at home, small companies with offices, and go on up to medium-sized firms and large concerns that are global in scope. As has been referenced many times in this book, the nature of services is that they are fragmented while rarely do only one or two large companies dominate in any given services sector. A thorough understanding of services competition therefore rests on a willingness to expend the time necessary to identify just where all the competitors are. And, throughout such an exercise, it is crucial to remember to see such competition as your customers or clients see it, not as you wish it to be.

Just What Is Your Industry Sector?

Before you can start tracking down your actual competitors, you will need to define just what you consider your industry sector to be. With services, given there is often a lack of clear-cut boundaries between what firms do or don't offer, this task can be time-consuming.

Take the exhibit service business as an example. Just where does this sector begin and end? Within exhibit services, there may be firms offering meeting planning services, display installation and dismantling services, graphic design for booths, staffing of booths, trucking and shipping services, freight forwarding and customs broker services, and more. The hotels and convention centers where such events are held are also part of the mix, as are the associations or other groups sponsoring the event. And, it is not a given that all these components function as discrete entities. Some larger exhibit service firms may offer a "total solution" encompassing booth design through set-up and knock-down, while others just handle the graphics or the shipping. Even worse, it is not a given that any one firm in the exhibit service business will stick with its defined turf. The fact of left-field competition may engineer a merger or alliance of several smaller firms into one behemoth. Or, a long-established supplier may suddenly introduce a range of new, innovative display services, which quickly eclipses other firms in the eyes of the customer. With services, rather than visualize a sector as a circle with a firm rim, think of it as a pulsating or mutating blob, whose edges are constantly shifting.

Or, to take adult continuing education, here is another services sector with mutable boundaries. If you are a provider of high-end seminars and conferences, like the American Management Association, catering to business people wishing to upgrade while holding down their current jobs, just where do you draw the line around your sector? Remember, undertaking such an analysis is not a good time to be a snob; just because you charge $2,000 or $3,000 for a program does not mean the prospective customers establish such a threshold and only consider similar offerings. You may need to take a whole spectrum of competing services into consideration: from university-based weekend or week-long programs going for $5,000, $10,000, or more, on down through less expensive commercial seminars, programs tacked onto industry annual conferences, community college courses, tele-education, learning packages created by business publications such as *Inc.*, and the mail-order diploma outfits. Although the services each offers and the price charged by each differs dramatically, all such organizations are still competing for the same pool of customers and the same pool of funds. As with the Blockbuster Video example cited in Chapter 2, keeping an open mind is essential to competing effectively.

Determining the extent of any service sector therefore takes time. For the best results from intelligence gathering efforts, it may be wise, at the start of the exercise, to use the broadest possible definition. Some of the ways to sort the wheat from the chaff of possible competitors will be discussed later in Part 2.

Finding High-Profile Competitors

Once you've begun to establish some boundaries, the next step is to scope out just who the competitors might be. In some services sectors, you may be fortunate in that at least some of the traditional competitors are what is known as "high profile." This is particularly true in sectors where the larger firms advertise extensively; sectors such as management consulting, executive recruitment, legal services, and accounting are examples of where it is easy enough to identify the higher profile players in the industry. But once you have identified the obvious, it will probably be more time-consuming to track down competitors who do not have such a public face. It's probably important, in this context, to be aware of any of the left-field competition referred to in Chapter 7 for many services, your competition may not be found within your geographic territory but rather in more far-flung points. This is true for the adult education sector mentioned above, as customers avail themselves of course providers located overseas. Or, competition may be buried within a group, such as an association, or within a company that operates in a seemingly different industry, as discussed in the case of ADP in Chapter 7.

Scoping out the boundaries of a sector is even easier if there is some degree of regulation and certification. Law, accounting, management consulting, executive search, health care providers, and travel agencies are just a few examples of services sectors that require practitioners to either have certain designations to practice or require them to be registered with a professional or regulatory body. If you operate a service firm in such a sector, you likely already know about such requirements and know where such groups are located. You may even automatically receive directories or have access to Web sites that list other practitioners. This will allow you ready access to identifying the universe of providers and deciding where to establish the beginning and end of your sector.

Finding Low-Profile Competition

More often, you will be in a services sector where none of your traditional competitors will be particularly visible, while other forms of competition, such as customers or influencers, will be even more widely dispersed and hidden. In sectors where vendors or suppliers are well established and the customer base is readily identifiable, marketing and selling services rests on word-of-mouth or on direct marketing and direct selling, meaning that the service providers—your hypothetical competition at this point in your inquiry—do not have to do much advertising or otherwise go about raising their profile in the public domain. The way the low-profile nature of an industry can thwart ready study of competition quickly raised itself as a stumbling block during an investigation into the merchandising services business. A retailer, with its own captive merchandising force, was interested in learning about the breadth and scope of merchandising services provided by independent, stand-alone merchandising service companies. Such companies maintain field forces of merchandisers, individuals who go into retail stores to keep a manufacturer's products well displayed and well stocked. They rotate stock, replenish it when it runs low, prepare displays of seasonal merchandise, such as at Christmas or Valentine's Day, and otherwise ensure that the manufacturer's brand stays competitive. Merchandisers are used in the retail industry for products as diverse as diapers, drug sundries, consumer electronics, greeting cards, and hosiery. The retailer with the captive force wanted to know: Where are all the other providers? What services do they offer? How many staff do they employ?

Identifying these service firms took some time. The Yellow Pages telephone directories were consulted for major cities, but, in each, no more than four or five merchandising companies were listed. Ads were then scanned in the newspapers, as classified advertising is the way merchandising services companies recruit new merchandising staff.

This turned up the odd name here and there but was not very fruitful. Searches were next run on publicly available online databases, such as DIALOG; print directories were also scanned manually. These searches proved the most productive: a list of 50 or so companies was generated, but only after the inapplicable had been eliminated—a large number of general stores and skate sharpening services turned up on the list! It was only when research moved to the interview phase, that the "mother lode" was found. A casual remark by someone at one of the identified merchandising companies revealed the existence of the National Association of Retail Merchandising Services (NARMS) and this organization's database of merchandisers nationwide; this was where most of the merchandise services companies were "hiding." Once all these steps had been undertaken, there was some assurance that most of the major firms had been identified and the industry located.

Finding Hidden Competition

The key role of a national group in this example also suggests the need to check out the hidden or left-field competition discussed in Chapter 7 that may be lurking at an association. Whenever a service firm sets out to identify its competitors, it needs to be aware of the presence and role of any industry associations in offering a competitive force. This can be particularly true in services sectors such as market research—many associations do offer fee-based research services to their members—and event planning services; many associations will provide a range of services in support of their annual national conference. This may include exhibitor services and even management; rather than contracting with an outside vendor, the association goes into do-it-yourself mode and blocks the availability of this market to for-profit service suppliers, by way of exclusive agreements with select providers. Even the legal and accounting services sectors are not immune to such hidden competition.

It may even be necessary to play sleuth to identify where the boundaries of your industry sector are set. A few years ago, Aetna, the insurance company, decided to introduce a new piece of software for its Administrative Services Only (ASO) account base. Prior to the launch,

Aetna wanted to learn which competitors it would face and how many. The assumption was that any competing ASO software would come from other insurers. Investigation of the market and the providers revealed that other insurers (Aetna's traditional competitors) were not the source of competition—few had any thoughts of developing stand-alone ASO packages—but that a dozen or more smaller software development companies were. Studying the competition therefore had to take a detour and showed Aetna it would be pitted against an array of unknown factors, once it did launch its ASO software. Here was a case where providers of a particular piece of software were not readily identifiable as such without a lot of digging and investigation. Providing ASO software was not the primary business objective of such firms, and so they did not list the availability of this software in any of their public information. Only by phoning up and discussing, with each company, what its capabilities were could any intentions to provide software for ASO applications be identified. This suggests that tapping multiple sources is a must to arrive at a complete picture.

Public Faces, Private Lives

How all the various avenues of intelligence must be utilized to truly be able to say you have explored your sector is illustrated in this example of an investigation into what are known as voice personals.

The voice personals business has a very public face from a customer's perspective—alternative weekly newspapers, globally, carry personals classifieds, and the Web now provides an electronic presence—but the companies running the services are hard to find. This is a case where the "product"—as it's known in the interactive voice response (IVR) industry, or service is not as hard to spot: there is a product for straight adults, one for gays, one for lesbians, one for people seeking platonic relationships with either same or opposite sex, one for specific ethnic groups (e.g., Hispanic in the United States), and so on.

Finding out about the companies behind the Web sites or the classifieds is another matter, and searches were complicated because many providers were taking advantage of technology and running as virtual or, at least, decentralized entities. Some had offices, full-time staff, and more tangible presences while others were little more than "smoke and mirrors." To study each company fully and understand its strengths and weaknesses meant moving beyond the public face of the industry. Often, Web sites or newspaper ads only offered 800 numbers that went to the call centers supporting the service and not to the head or corporate office. Personnel at the 800 numbers often either did not know the headquarters number or refused to provide it.

Unraveling the industry involved abandoning online information as a source and turning to more prosaic "Old Economy" sources. Searches at the state level, using the scant information already obtained, turned up incorporation papers. Where owners of the IVR businesses were known by name, searches of credit records were undertaken. Uniform Commercial Code (UCC) records were also tapped. After some diligent sleuthing, enough data had been gathered to pin down who the traditional competitors were and where they could be found. This enabled the investigators to size the industry sector and decide which companies merited further attention.

Customer and Influencer Competition

Although identifying other providers—and the possibility of traditional competitors—is an important step to take, if yours is like many service firms, you may often be a sole-source supplier and only infrequently in competitive bid situations. This means that the boundaries of your sector need to be drawn accordingly, two of the more pressing forms of competition to deal with will be customer-origin and influencer competition.

While it is easier to spot where this competition likely resides—you do, after all, know who your customers are—this ease of recognition should not lull you into a false sense of security. It is important even when the relationship is long standing to keep tabs on personnel changes; your direct contact may remain in her job, but if she has a new boss, who has other ideas on how the services you offer should be procured, the dynamics at your customer organization will change and there will be no "givens" in the relationship. Changes in overall ownership also need to be monitored; if an American-based company is bought by another organization in Germany or Japan, a new source of competition may enter the fray if the new owners consider expenditures on your type of service a "waste." Even long-established relationships of 10 or 20 years are vulnerable to being unseated by such competitive forces.

To keep informed, you obviously have the customers themselves as a front-line resource. But gathering additional public-domain information is also an important confirming step; notices in the business press, the annual reports of customers, and ensuring you are on their mailing lists to receive press releases are just three avenues to feeling the pulse of developments at customers or clients.

The rapidity of change in the business world also suggests it is only common-sense to keep informed—and in touch with—influencers at customer or client organizations. Knowing who else works in your primary contact's department, knowing who has sign-off on projects, knowing the customer's procedure for approvals, are all important ways of keeping on top of where the competition lurks. Such knowledge can be especially valuable when your contact leaves. This way, you can keep in touch with influencers and ensure they put in a good word for your firm once there is a new hire in the contact position. And all these tactics will prove invaluable with prospective clients; scoping out the sources of competition *before* you present your services will ensure a more rapid and successful introduction and a greater chance you will land some business.

Government Source Competition

Just as customer and influencer competition should be easy to locate, government is highly visible. However, the element of government competition that a service provider needs to be aware of is that it can be silent, if not downright sneaky, in how it comes into existence and penetrates your sector.

In the examples of government competition in Chapter 4, neither the U.S. nor Canadian federal governments went to either the lab testing or telemarketing sectors and said, "We're thinking of setting up shop in your industry; do you mind?" If your firm is frequently in the running for government work, even if there has historically been no competition from a government-affiliated entity, vigilance is required to spot this form of competition before it becomes troublesome.

Tracking government news Web sites or any publications originating with government are just two ways to do this, as is belonging to associations—such as the National Federation of Independent Business (NFIB) in the United States or the Canadian Federation of Independent Business (CFIB) in Canada—to keep in the loop on any alerting services they have.

Where to Look for Intelligence About Where Competitors Are

Several of the sources that can be tapped to both define your industry sector and identify the universe of providers have already been referenced in this chapter, but a recap will allow for review of these and consideration of others.

To scope out the boundaries of your industry and decide who is or isn't a candidate for inclusion—and a potential competitor—look to the buyer's guide issues of the major trade magazines serving the industry along with any exhibitors catalogs available from the leading trade shows. Tap all the associations and self-regulating bodies in the sector for further lists or directories, whether in print or Web based. Don't overlook any referral databases whether run by an association or a for-profit group. If these sources aren't turning up much material, you can also consider for-purchase mailing lists from the various list providers, such as American Business Information, to get you started.

Another worthwhile avenue to explore is paid advertising; scanning for ads, particularly those placed in publications catering to customers, may allow you to add to your universe of providers and, within this, traditional competitors. A check of the large display ads and smaller classified ads in leading business newspapers, such as the *Wall Street Journal*, the *Financial Times*, or the *Globe and Mail*, will lead you to names. Government records of registered businesses plus the phone directories for any locations where you operate will lend additional rigor to your search.

Identifying the sources of customer/client, influencer, and government competition should be an easier step; with these competitive forces, ensuring you are on the right mailing lists or checking the right Web sites or databases regularly will keep you up-to-date on events that could affect you.

How to Use the CI You Gather

How you use this intelligence will depend, to some extent, on what you find. Once you have material to help define the boundaries of your sector, you can use this to identify where your own business fits into the scheme of things and how you measure up within the industry as a whole. This may lead to consideration of ways you can innovate to become more competitive or a bigger player. Identifying all the likely competitors will enable you to determine how wide-ranging your ongoing intelligence efforts need to be and the resources you have to devote to the task. If several key providers—and possible competitors—are geographically dispersed, then doing CI may involve a greater expenditure and more time than if everyone is close to your location.

As for which traditional competitors you need to track, Chapters 9 and 10, about strategy and the service offering, will help you pin down those companies you need to track all the time, as opposed to those you need to follow some of the time.

Finding Your Competition

- For regulated professions, tap into lists and sources maintained by regulatory bodies.

- Associations may also have directories and databases.

- Buyers Guide or "directory issues" of trade magazines provide further starting points.

- Purchased mailing lists from list brokers may yield more providers.

- Scanning publications for ads, appointment notices, and changes in corporate ownership is also an important step.

- Obtaining annual reports can keep your knowledge current.

- Checking Web sites when applicable and contacting providers directly are other steps you can take.

CHAPTER 9

What's Their Strategy?

One of the keys to understanding your traditional competitors and, by association, the broader competitive environment, is to study each company's strategy and determine: Where are these companies going? What are they trying to achieve? In *Competitive Strategy*, Michael Porter writes, "Every firm competing in an industry has a competitive strategy, whether explicit or implicit." Porter then describes how such strategy may have been thought out, the result of a detailed planning process, or it may have come into existence in an ad hoc fashion, merely as an outcome of what the firm or its component departments happen to be doing.

Spotting Competitors' Strategies

Determining strategy in the services sector is more of a challenge than it is for goods-producing businesses (although it can sometimes be challenging for products) simply because a service firm's strategy can be changed so quickly. It is yet one more aspect of a company's activities that can remain low profile or nearly invisible, revealed only to the customers or clients. Competitive intelligence work designed to probe issues of strategy needs to take into account the buried nature of much strategy in services and will have to rely on methods that allow you to probe a moving target. The other reason it is important to learn about traditional competitors' strategies and how the broader environment sees these organizations is that their strategy reflects upon you. If competitors have decided to position themselves as a high-end provider of services, the crème de la crème of the industry, the unspoken message conveyed may be that your firm is a provider of low-end services or not much good. This message, once picked up by customers and influencers, can have a detrimental effect on the type of work you are asked to perform and the level of fees you can charge for your services.

To return to the case of Lasik Vision, discussed in Chapter 6, it is suspected that the operators of other laser vision correction centers probably wished they had spent more time watching this company's strategy. Once Lasik Vision embarked on its low-cost, high-volume strategy, any provider of a higher cost procedure began to be tarnished in the public view. Had other clinics seized the initiative sooner and taken control of the agenda—by developing a strategy that, perhaps, emphasized higher quality control or better follow-up after procedures had been performed—they might have avoided being dragged into a downward pricing spiral, which became detrimental to all players in the industry.

This suggests that early intelligence efforts around strategy need to focus on what type of firm your traditional competitors want to be. Like much intelligence work, the best answers to this question will come from careful assembly of materials originating with your traditional competitors, such as image advertisements and brochures. This is certainly true of the larger service firms that can afford more for advertising budgets. Such ads are frequently run when the firm has regrouped and renamed as in the case where Andersen Consulting, spun off from its accounting firm partners, changed its name to Accenture. A sizeable advertising campaign was run to announce what the new firm would offer and, by inference, its strategy.

Monitoring competitors' strategies can also tell you how they're responding to factors of competition, such as "left-field competition" referenced in Chapter 7. When commoditization, for example, starts to downgrade specific services, such as the tax and auditing services referenced, how do firms respond? In the case of accountants, they may develop a new strategy to partner with other firms, such as law firms, or move into more "boutique" areas, such as forensic accounting. (Such differentiation will also be discussed later in this chapter and in Chapter 12.)

Spotting your traditional competitor's initiative in response to commoditization may also be the first tip-off you have that such a change is affecting your industry. In this way, competitive intelligence about other firms' strategies is a valuable tool to answer questions such as: How has our industry changed? What is going on in the marketplace? And what should we do about it?

Positioning Tactics

The strategy used by a service business will often be reflected in its positioning statement; as well as looking into strategy, an investigation of positioning will also tell you how the firm wants the world—or more particularly its customers or clients—to see it. This was the challenge for the president of a lawn care services company who had a franchise territory. Business had built easily in the first three years, but growth had since plateaued. Of interest to him, as a tool for going forward, was understanding how his competitors, who were either independents or ran franchises for other companies, were doing in the same territory. Had their growth also plateaued? Or were they still adding new accounts? (He was aware he'd lost some of his own accounts to these competitors.)

Part of figuring out what was going on and how this affected his business rested on probing his traditional competitors' positioning. How were they presenting lawn care to the prospective customers? Were they positioning the environmental advantages, the safety of their approaches and treatment methods to an increasingly ecologically minded clientele? Or did they stress the time-saving, worry-free nature of their programs to harried, dual-income two parent households with no time to maintain their lawns?

By collecting up competitors' literature and deducing their positioning (when such was not explicitly stated) plus cross-checking this against his territory and lost account records, the lawn care services operator was able to identify how competitors had positioned themselves in different neighborhoods and how successful they had been. This allowed him to re-segment his territory and position his own business more profitably to the various subsegments in the market, meaning his investment in gathering CI paid off.

Sometimes positioning is harder to determine, especially when a category of service is emerging and the players themselves are trying to decide what their positioning will be. This was true when, a few years ago, the pharmaceutical giant, Bayer Corporation, decided it should start a new venture and position this into the wellness market. While Bayer might be considered a more traditional manufacturing concern, the goal of the company in undertaking this initiative was to move beyond traditional products and branch out into related services under the wellness umbrella. The company therefore set out to look at how other pharmaceutical firms perceived wellness and how this category was generally perceived within all segments of the health care sector. What Bayer found was that, due to the newness of the interest in wellness, there was little agreement as to what the term meant while most large corporations were as lost as it was in deciding how to position themselves under the wellness umbrella. If yours is a newer or more innovative service, you may encounter a similar lack of definition among industry players although, on the plus side, you may find you have scope to define your sector as well as your own business' position.

Mission and Vision Statements Can Be Revealing

A further tactic to learn about traditional competitors' strategies is to look for mission statements or slogans in any advertising they place or in the literature they produce.

Many in the intelligence field find mission statements useful for forecasting their competitors' behaviors, not to mention predicting how other competitive factors, such as customers or influencers, may respond. Mission statements reveal how a company thinks and answer the question: What does it believe? Another useful indicator from a mission statement is: What values will the company apply to decision-making?[1] Although law firms for many years had very staid images, in recent years many have turned to a mission statement or slogan to convey their positioning and by association what they offer to their clients. Take, for example, the statement on the letterhead of the law firm Fraser Milner Casgrain operating in Canada, which is, simply, "Business. Advice. Success." The intent of the vision statement is to indicate that this firm, and they alone, have the capabilities to act on the concepts expressed in the statement. Similar objectives are expressed on the letterhead of financial consultants Markowitz & McNaughton: "Helping executives know the next move." The vision offered by the Futures Group on its marketing materials is "Building Robust Strategies." Similarly, California-based communications consulting firm MedComm Solutions explains it is "Raising the Standards of Performance in Medical Communications," while contract research organization (CRO) APEX International, in Taiwan, states: "Our vision is to establish the most professional and competitive CRO team in the Asia-Pacific region." And in Australia, the MindShifts Group lets us know it offers "A Smarter Way to Compete."

This is why, when the vice president of corporate development of North American Life Insurance Company was tasked with formulating a new mission statement for his employer, he set out to gather the mission statements of several other insurers to find out how they were positioning themselves and what these statements might suggest about their overall strategy. The process took about three weeks—this was in the pre-Internet era—but the results were worth the wait. Some insurers had unwieldy statements while others had concise 5- to 10-word missions. The vice president was then able to spread these out to gain a "bird's eye view" of his competitors, then re-group them by key themes. Some companies were positioning around their comprehensiveness of product or their pricing while others were repositioning themselves around the "solutions" they offered. The real benefit to North American Life was in spotting the gaps and locating the "unstaked turf" so it could use its own mission statement to distance the company from the competition.

Shifts in strategy can sometimes be signaled in subtle changes to a service firm's mission statement. Such was true for Trammell Crow, a real estate developer. Prior to 1989, the company's mission statement or vision read, "To be the premier customer-driven real estate company in the U.S." After this time, the statement read, "To be the premier customer-driven real estate *services* company in the U.S." The insertion of the word "services" indicating a new focus and a range of activities beyond basic real estate development. In fact, Trammell Crow had moved more squarely into being a service firm; sometimes, mission statement analysis can tip you off to left-field competition when an erstwhile goods-producer, perhaps recognizing manufacturing is only a small part of its business, is now migrating into services—and thus into direct competition with you.

The Branding Impetus

Equally part of strategic maneuvering is the way service businesses will try to copy the goods-producing sector by turning themselves into a brand. While brand names for products, such as Coca-Cola and Pepsi (along with Kleenex and Xerox), are well-known words which have become synonymous with their products—this practice has been less well followed in the services sector. Most attempts at branding have been undertaken, not surprisingly, by ad agencies and the like; should a traditional competitor of yours in the services sector be attempting to brand itself, it is important to identify this via competitive intelligence work so the competitor doesn't gain too much of an ascendancy in the customer's mind and start to exert undue control over the marketplace.

You can spot such branding initiatives via traditional competitors advertising, brochures, a change in corporate logo or corporate colors, along with attempts by them to gain control of the agenda in your industry sector. The sector's main annual conference may be an opportune time for a competitor to try to stake out its turf via a branding campaign; watch for sponsorships of lunches, coffee breaks, and other conference events as a signal this is what they are up to.

The Business of Differentiation

Initiatives with positioning and branding are, in many respects, simply window dressing for the real underpinning of strategy and that is what a particular services firm does to set itself apart. It is within the arena of differentiation that services providers of all persuasions try to distance themselves from their traditional competitors.[2] One method frequently employed by larger firms is to differentiate by geographical scope. Globalization in many sectors of the economy has brought about the need for supporting firms, such as those offering professional services, to provide seamless services across geographical boundaries to their manufacturing and distributing clients. Whereas, at one time, even member firms of one of the Big Five accounting or management consulting firms tended to operate autonomously, integration is now on the rise so that geographical boundaries become irrelevant.[3]

Their Expertise Versus Yours

But not all firms have the resources to provide services internationally and so a further way professional service firms differentiate themselves is by expertise. This differentiation rests on the supposedly superior quality of the firm's work. Such entities are often referred to as boutiques, firms with a narrow focus and deep expertise. In the United States, one example of this differentiation is the emergence of firms specializing in personal injury law. Other boutique-type enterprises would be peopled mainly by tax specialists (instead of broader accounting services) or by forensic accountants only. Firms in the executive recruitment field may differentiate themselves by specializing in one or two industries, such as high-tech. Ad agencies may devote themselves strictly to the retail industry.

Another way service firms may differentiate by expertise is by focusing on particular types of client. This may include accounting firms that specialize in serving family-owned businesses or law firms that handle strictly entertainers as clients. Within financial services, this differentiation of expertise shows up in the separate private banking organizations, within each financial services institution, which are designed to cater to people who meet certain net-worth criteria.

In studying the expertise differentiations of other providers, it is also beneficial to assess when such specializations might prove detrimental to your competitors. One of the risks in being a boutique firm is that fashions can change; not so long ago, quality management and quality circles were key buzzwords within the overall management consulting field. Now, quality is a better established principle and so consultants catering to people needing quality programs are less in demand. For a time "supply-chain management" was a hot topic but that, too, has cooled down, leaving specialist or boutique firms scrambling to find new niches where they can reinvent their expertise. Similarly, while e-commerce was an extremely hot field in the last few years of the 20th century, indications are that demand in this area of specialization will also flatten in the years ahead. Lawyers who specialize in insolvency may have lean years during good times, as might any consultants specializing in crisis management.

Tacit Knowledge

Differentiation around expertise has been heightened in recent years by the growing emphasis on Knowledge Management (KM) at services firms. Companies have been investing heavily in finding ways to make better use of what they already know—sometimes referred to as "tacit knowledge"—and cross-utilizing the expertise and know-how of their staff especially when scattered across multiple sites around the world. Sometimes, these KM networks will be informal, brought about by greater awareness within the firm or more dialogue; at other times, they will result from formal efforts using technology and developing databases. Large management consulting firms like Ernst & Young have particularly made strides in this area; while their resources may not be within the scope of smaller firms, other service organizations can at least study how it's done and modify the ideas to fit.[4]

Mix and Match for Competitive Advantage

Another way service firms attempt to develop a strategy, based on differentiation, is in the service mix; what they actually offer to clients and how the parts are mixed together. This strategy can best be described as a "one-stop shopping" strategy that allows clients the peace of mind of only having to deal with one service firm provider rather than several. Historically, the service mix strategy and the breadth of service underlying it was only available to the larger service firms but, nowadays, thanks to the increasing role of alliances and partnerships, small to mid-sized service firms in a range of disciplines have been moving into the arena of offering one-stop shopping for their clients. From a competitive point of view, it is important to determine if your traditional competitors have indeed entered into such arrangements and determine where this leaves you, if you do not participate in an alliance.

Ways to Deliver

Mode of delivery is a further way in which service businesses develop strategies to seek competitive advantage. This strategy often amounts to no more than delivering the service in a way that appeals to the client. The actual content of what is delivered by one firm may differ very little from what its competitors might do. This strategy can rest on the access clients enjoy to senior partners in the firm and promises that no juniors will do any of the work. Other facets involve how the firm manages the client relationship in between assignments, so as to maximize customer retention. From a competitive point of view, looking into these issues is important because it illustrates how ripe customers might be to consider another supplier or whether or not the previous provider, your traditional competitor, has such a "lock" on the client that landing any new business here will be next to impossible.

How They Price

One of the last ways in which service firms differentiate themselves is by price. One of the dangers with pricing is that attempts to be a low-cost provider of services may indicate that the services are cut-rate or inferior to those offered by someone who charges more. All the strategies and positioning in the world won't be of much value if the firm is not successful financially and in other ways. One of the next tasks for a competitive intelligence campaign around the issue of strategy is to find out if all these tactics by other providers in your sector are actually paying off. (These issues are discussed in more detail in Chapter 14.)

Acquisitions And Alliances

The role of partnerships and other "marriages" between service firms have been referenced already, but their significance in determining the strategy of competitors merits further discussion.

When competition intensifies and markets stagnate, many service firms seek out either partnerships or more permanent arrangements in the form of mergers. Such a trend to services marriages has already gained momentum in financial services, in law, and in management consulting, as when Price Waterhouse merged with Coopers & Lybrand to form PriceWaterhouseCoopers.

Apart from yielding some tongue-twister names, such maneuvers can indicate changes in strategy along with the emergence of a competitive force with more clout. Nor is this a game played only by giants. If you are the operator of a smaller service firm that has historically competed only with firms of a similar size, the acquisition of one of these firms by a larger entity can signal trouble ahead. Within the bosom of a larger parent, the once-small competitor now has access to more resources and therefore can take a stronger, higher profile in the marketplace.[5]

This is another development where tracking customer and influencer competition, to find out their perceptions, is so key; if they welcome the change, it may spell trouble for your firm. If they are concerned about dealing with a much larger entity, then it may be appropriate timing for you to counteract the competitive force by doing some repositioning of your own, stressing the advantages you offer, as a smaller, independent company.

Even when acquisitions seem almost strange and don't make sense, they merit consideration as an indicator of "the shape of things to come." A few years ago, Cendant Corporation, which offers various services in sectors as diverse as real estate and emergency service to motorists, purchased an interactive voice response (IVR) company in the voice personals business. From a strategic point of view, it was hard to see why Cendant wanted to enter such a dissimilar business. The reasons became apparent on investigation; Cendant had purchased the IVR firm less for its business than for its database. Plans were afoot to use all of Cendant's databases to build new business and the IVR database was just one more piece of the puzzle; a strategy was taking shape that would rest on this consolidated direct marketing resource and take Cendant into new areas.

While strategy, branding, and positioning may seem to represent more vague aspects of competition and therefore competitive intelligence gathering, as referenced above, if you do not investigate these issues, you leave yourself exposed to gaining an inappropriate reputation or image in the marketplace as clients and prospective clients infer from any of your competitors strategies and positioning that the opposite must be true for you.

Where to Look for Intelligence About Strategy

Probing competing firms' strategies, no less than other forms of intelligence, rests on being a good "ferret" and retrieving material from a range of sources.

Advertisements, especially the kind known as "image" ads, are an important source of intelligence as are brochures and other pieces of material emanating from the competitors themselves. New logos, new designs for the letterhead, and new business cards for the staff can also tip you off to changes in strategy; these changes can be subtle, so don't discard any material that comes into your possession even if it does look remarkably similar to the business card or letterhead you already have. If your traditional competitors have recently hired a new ad agency or a public relations firm, this can indicate a major campaign is planned, which could easily be to support a new strategy, an attempt at branding, or a different positioning statement.

Another way you may be able to gather intelligence about this aspect of your competitors' activities is via the annual conference in your sector or similar meetings held by groups to which major customers belong. How your competitors present themselves, any change in the tone of their behavior and similar shifts can be early indicators of plans they have afoot.

When your competitors are smaller, the only way to pick up on some of these issues is to be on their mailing lists so you receive letters and other promotional items they send out. Make sure, however, that the people opening the mail at your firm know the significance of such items and don't discard them as junk mail!

Other shifts in strategy may be detected if you suddenly get a call from a customer you have not dealt with for a long time who suddenly has lost a supplier (one of your competitors). If the competitor has decided to reposition itself as only serving certain industries or only certain sizes of company, you may be the beneficiary of a new piece of business along with a tip-off that your competitor is beating up a new path. And any time there is a merger or alliance, or a change in leadership at a competing firm, keep alert to accompanying changes in strategy—and how they will change the marketplace.

What To Do With the CI You Gather

The suggestion has already been made that a service firm ignores strategic maneuvering by competitors at its peril; your firm may be "slotted" into a spot you don't want or have its reputation skewed by the initiatives of competitors.

As you gather intelligence about strategy, positioning, and branding, you need to create a map or grid showing where your competitors want to be and seeing where this leaves you. If all your traditional competitors are crowding the premium, high-value-added position, do you want to join them or is there a more profitable position for you? If they are all pursuing certain industry segments for customers, what opportunities can you find for your firm? And if they threaten to crowd you out of markets where you want to be, how can you fight back? These questions are just some of the ones you can answer with the CI you have gathered.

References

1. "What You Can Learn From Your Competitors' Mission Statements." *Competitive Intelligence Review*. Winter 1995: 35-40.
2. "Five Strategies To Make a Professional Services Firm Stand Out." *The Globe and Mail*. November 6, 2000: M1.
3. "Globalization and Nationalism in a Multinational Accounting Firm: The Case of Opening New Markets in Eastern Europe." *Accounting, Organizations and Society*. 1998: Vol 23, Issues 5/6.
4. "Knowledge Management at Ernst & Young." Stanford Graduate School of Business. September 1997: 19 + exhibits.
5. "Merging Professional Service Firms." *Organization Science*. May 1994: 239-257.

Learning Their Strategy

• Systematically monitor your traditional competitors' ads and promotional materials to learn when they are changing direction.

- Attend events where traditional competitors are exhibitors or sponsors to spot changes in logos, branding, mission statements, etc.

- Once you have identified traditional competitors, scan their Web sites, or obtain their brochures to monitor their strategy.

- Keep track of new suppliers, partners, or other relationships your traditional competitors are forming; these also signal their strategic intentions.

- Find ways to be added to traditional competitors' mailing lists to receive regular updates.

CHAPTER 10

What Are They Selling?

In a goods-producing business, studying the product is easy. It can be spotted on store shelves, viewed in catalogs, ordered and examined, sourced from a distributor; it can be touched, seen, felt, smelled, and tasted. It can be measured, weighed, taken apart, and reassembled. Not so the service. It is largely invisible and often elastic, changing to suit each customer. The high level of customization in services renders many comparisons academic: How do you compare what you offer to services that are more dissimilar than similar? For example, one lawyer, handling a real estate closing, may provide a very different service than any other lawyer. While there are basics in common to all real estate closings—certain tasks that have to be performed, certain documents that have to be filed—what a lawyer provides over and above this distinguishes her service in the eyes of the customer. The attention to detail the lawyer offers, the level of experience in real estate law, the depth of advice provided, and any services that are included *gratis*, can produce disparities when comparing one real estate closing to another.

What Is a Service?

This suggests that any competitive intelligence gathering exercise will only bear fruit if the investigating company first decides what a service is. Let us suppose an executive recruitment firm wants to study competition: Is the service they offer and wish to study at other firms their core activity of interviewing candidates for a job? Or does it encompass all aspects of what is offered to a client, from initial meetings prior to taking on the assignment through the final selection and placement of a candidate? And, in the event it falls somewhere in between, where and how do you draw boundaries? Another complicating factor lies in aspects of services that are subjective. Let us suppose you include client meetings as part of the service and the consultant is having a good day, the sun is shining, and the client has a great time at lunch: should such elements be evaluated or ignored?

It is, perhaps, for this reason that many service businesses try to objectify what they do and refer to their service as a "work product." This may cut things down to size. The case of an employment law firm, whose work had been called into question, illustrates this. The firm built its case on the concept of its work product: the sum total of the advice and expertise gained in the area of immigration law, which they had applied to a particular client's situation. Once this work product had been passed on, the client had the firm's knowledge and could make use of it, independent of the firm. This raises a further facet of the service; in determining what you compete against, you will also need to remember that elements of the service both remain with the service provider *and* enter the possession of the customer.

Promise Versus Performance

Related to this is the point at which competition begins and ends in the client's mind, as raised in Chapter 2. If the client is evaluating firms *before* selecting a supplier, which is when such evaluations usually occur, then the actual service, which has not yet been performed, cannot be compared with what is available in the market. This is why a firm's *potential* to come through is what is assessed. For the purposes of gathering competitive intelligence, you need to have a dual focus: services performed by competitors in the past plus their potential to perform them in the future. Both form the basis of competition. Such potential to perform will often be indicated by proposals, quotes, or other written material, along with the firm's track record. The service provider can only be assessed (for a first time supplier) on the basis of services performed for *other clients*; that such other clients may be competitors to the company making the evaluation further complicates the picture! From a competitive point of view, this suggests that it may be as important to study your competitors' business development activities and their proposal writing skills as it is to define where their service begins and ends.

Relying on References

The fact that the purchase of a service involves buying something that does not yet exist raises another facet of the service to investigate, and that is the role of references in shaping the services purchase decision. If the client is only able to make comparisons on the basis of a firm's promise, then references are key. And just who might your competitors be giving as their references? Although the issue of who they know will be examined in more detail in Chapter 15, it is important to consider the prestige or otherwise of your traditional competitors' referees. In an environment when the service can only be evaluated after purchase, especially when the service will be highly customized, the decision may turn on the type of reference given for each of the suppliers under consideration. If your references are middle managers while your competitors offer high level executives as theirs, you may be at a disadvantage. Or, if a competitors' references are less busy and call the prospective customer back sooner, they may land the business at your expense. Such superficial attributes only touch on this issue; what their references say compared to yours, the content of the reference, is another dimension.

Getting to Know Basic Service

Some of the complexities of studying services and making comparisons between competing firms arose during an investigation of private banking services. These services are offered by financial institutions to cater to their wealthier clients. Private banking is set up for this purpose and often operates as a "bank within a bank." Separate branches, which look more like private offices, are often lavishly appointed. However, in the case of the institution trying to learn more about several competitors' offerings, defining just where the service began and ended, and how it was perceived by the clients and prospective clients, was not an easy task.

As a first step, the promotional brochures of each competitor were obtained and analyzed. This indicated a wide range of services available under the private banking umbrella at each target organization. Already, an apples-to-apples comparison did not exist. Then, sample client statements were obtained, which revealed a similar range of disparities. Due to the clients' wealth, it was possible for each institution to offer a tailored statement, as it was easy to absorb the cost of customization.

Next, attention turned to where the services were available. Some institutions had located their private banking centers close to the residential areas inhabited by wealthy people while others had opted for downtown locations in the financial centers. Again, the "what" that each competitor was selling was quite different—and also indicated different underlying strategies. Some banks obviously positioned themselves as catering to the "idle rich," while others wanted to serve the "working rich." Examining competing private banking services meant grappling with several layers, which made up the service.

While studying basic services, your firm also needs to look at how focused or otherwise your competitors are. The tendency is for the larger service providers to be focused, to build and offer services based strictly on certain expertises and track records and not to try and do too much. With smaller providers, you may encounter less focus and a firm that offers everything from soup to nuts. While this is the competitor's choice, the temptation for such firms to try and do everything can have unpleasant repercussions when they try to provide services for which they are not truly qualified.

This can be an important element of monitoring the new market entrants referenced in Chapter 5; as they try to build business, they may bite off more than they can chew and do damage among the customer base as discussed in Chapter 2. By identifying which providers are vulnerable to making this mistake, you can be armed to address any problems by way of customer contact and marketing initiatives.

The Lowdown on Value-Added Services

This ties into consideration one of the more common strategies used by service firms as concerns the actual service, especially when the competitive factor of commoditization (as discussed in Chapter 7) rears its head, and that is what's known as the "value-added" service.

In this way, companies that once offered a bare-bones tax and accounting service will migrate their services to a fuller scope, offering advice around business valuation, acquisitions and divestitures, shareholder value, and more. A travel services firm, rather than responding in a "step'n'fetchit" fashion by just making reservations or delivering tickets, will add value by price shopping for corporate clients, coordinating meeting travel, and moving to a role where they *anticipate* their customer needs.

An extension of this migration to value-added services concerns ways your traditional competitors may be attempting to establish what they do as the gold standard. Much as with the positioning and branding activities discussed in Chapter 9, at the service level competitors may be maneuvering to set up their particular service offering as the benchmark against which all others are compared.

This can lead to situations where customers and influencers start to find your service lacking: "What do you mean, you do not automatically include X in your service? Company ABC does." This can have a direct tie-in to how you price your services, as will be explored in Chapter 14. Failing to identify and deal with competitors' tactics to set themselves up as offering the gold standard can lead to erosion of your customer base and market share.

Customization

Another facet of services is customization: This goes beyond even the concept of value-added services to the capability to tailor each and every piece of work to the customer's requirements. The fact that service can be so readily customized within the scope of a firm's standard offering is another complicating factor when trying to study and compare companies in any given sector.

Finding out about competitors' levels of customization was key learning for a firm of business brokers intent on expanding its markets geographically. While listing and selling a business is the core service any business broker offers, the ways other providers added value and customized demonstrated the level of customer expectations and what the expansion-minded broker would have to do to compete more effectively.

Some other brokers went considerably beyond just listing a business and waiting for the calls to come in. They maintained databases of prospective purchasers or went out soliciting buyers. Others took this to a greater level of customization by treating each business transaction as a unique event; these brokers would research and identify prospective acquisitions for their clients and customize each client assignment rather than remaining in a reactive role. As a result, their service offering was more comprehensive.

Assessing Integrated Services

In attempting to compare the essence of your service to those of your competitors, especially the larger firms in your industry sector, it is also important to look at how they may be offering integrated services and doing an end-run around you in this way.

With the larger firms, such integrated services will likely pool the resources of several departments or locations under the same service umbrella. For example, if a client wishes to relocate a factory or its head office, a large management consulting firm can go beyond mere value-added services and offer what is known as a total solution. Location experts from the firm can be tapped to scout the new site, while legal or tax experts can assess the legal or financial implications of the move. If the objective is to gain better economies of scale then, no problem, the firm's information technology (IT) specialists can get to work, while its human resources team can help the client manage the people side of the move.

Nor is it enough to assess just your larger competitors in the area of integrated services. Some of your smaller competitors may be positioned to leapfrog over you by forming alliances to offer a similar scope of services, as was discussed in Chapter 9. In gathering intelligence about them, you need to be especially alert to such partnerships that may have been formed without a lot of fanfare.

What Are They Selling Today?

Finding out what a competitor is selling can often be complicated by the fact that the competitor may not wish you to know it is offering a particular service. This was one of the complicating factors in determining the scope of services offered under the moniker of "interim hotel management." This state of affairs comes into existence when hotels become what are known as distressed properties; the owners fall into default on loans, but the hotel has to keep going in the meantime. A profitable hotel chain, sensing a business opportunity to build upon some of its core expertise during a recession, decided to find out what competitors were offering in the way of management services to hotel properties in distress.

The initial assumption was that other hotel chains would be the main competitors, but this assumption proved false; this was another case where the competition was either hidden or of the left-field variety. Since in all cases banks are involved as lenders when hotel properties become distressed, it was decided that the financing parties would be a useful link to identifying the consultants or firms stepping in to manage the hotels. Another assumption; another wild goose chase! Many banks denied having any distressed properties on their books. Eventually, the loans officers who were dealing with hotels were tracked down, buried in what banks euphemistically call the Special Loans department.

This did lead to names of potential competitors for the hotel chain making the inquiry. Next, each of these companies had to be contacted; only a few had brochures (this was in the pre-Internet era). Then came the task of determining the actual services each player offered. Some, it seemed, were sole practitioners who did nothing but manage distressed hotel properties; theirs was a highly focused, niche service designed to keep the hotel going until a buyer could be found or the loans paid off. Other competitors were departments or consultants operating within a larger consulting firm; as well as providing interim management services, they would also act as brokers seeking buyers, or otherwise make matches to try to resolve the situation. And then there were a couple of hotel chains that provided interim management but with a view to turning the property around and buying the hotel.

In short, a typical services offering: dissimilar services from dissimilar providers but with a common objective—keeping the hotel going! Yet these were the competing services that the new market entrant, the hotel chain, would face, if and when it decided to branch out into interim hotel management.

When Their Service Bests Yours

Understanding a competitor's service is particularly important once it has landed a piece of business and you have not. You need to learn more as to why they were successful. All of the activities—the phone calls, meetings, lunches, presentations, proposals—that the competitor undertakes with the prospective client or clients, prior to a decision, represents part of what they are selling and what you are competing against. And, in amongst all this, you will have to be able to discern what particular feature struck home for each particular client; for example, in financial services, it is not a given that each pension plan sponsor will select a supplier for the same reason as any other pension plan sponsor. And you will also need to learn about any influencers at work behind the scenes. It is not a given that all the effort expended by each supplier was really evaluated. The decision as to where to place the funds may turn on connections at the board level, where someone gives the nod to a favorite.

What Will They Be Selling in the Future?

Finding out about what traditional competitors' services are offering today is only part of the equation of understanding what they are selling. The other half is finding out what they'll be selling tomorrow. To remain competitive, it is essential for your firm to gain a sense of this so you do not see a stampede of customers away from your door to a new offering from one of your competitors, or witness a loss of market potential as a competitor launches a copycat service to something you have introduced or are planning to sell.

A few years ago, Cooperators Data Services Ltd. (CDSL), the data management affiliate of The Cooperators Insurance Company, was in process of assessing business opportunities for future growth. An internal review of the company's expertise had led it to identifying local area network (LAN) management as a particular set of skills that might be marketable, independent of its insurer parent or, for that matter, the insurance industry.

At the time, LANs were still new, although other forms of data processing services were available on an outsourced basis. Along with identifying potential customers for the service, CDSL also wanted to know if any existing data processing services were also thinking of providing an outsourced LAN management service. But it needed to do so without "tipping its hand."

This meant the company had to conduct a series of investigations of all the "likely suspects" in its geographic markets. Their printed literature was sourced first, and then any advertising each company was doing, in print media, was studied. Then, the expertises of each firm, as evidenced by both service offering and the staff, was scrutinized. Those companies that seemed to either have existing expertise or that showed an aggressive expansion history were then contacted and key personnel interviewed.

This produced the findings that few had any inclination to offer outsource LAN management to the marketplace (and the customer research undertaken by CDSL also indicated their idea was premature; at the time, too few companies had a LAN or knew what one was). In spite of this, CDSL made good use of overall market intelligence gathered as it was able to shelve the idea for more favorable timing at a later date.

Where to Look for Intelligence About the Service

How then, can a company gather competitive intelligence about the services against which it competes? Since the service cannot be readily "plucked off the shelf" and examined, nor can it be reverse engineered—a common tactic used in the goods-producing sector—a services company has to employ a range of stratagems and tap multiple sources to begin to understand what comprises their competitors' services. An equally important part of this exercise is to manage expectations of results accordingly; it is unlikely that a services business will ever pin down all facets of its competitors' offering but must instead arrive at an understanding by deducing from the information that is available. The first deduction is what the competitor offers; the second is how the customers or clients perceive the offering.

One obvious route to the intelligence you need is to tap into existing clients or customers or, perhaps, the former clients or customers of the target competitors. If the parting of the ways between a competitor and the customer/client was not happy, the client or customer may have no qualms in sharing reports, proposals, brochures, and other insight about their former supplier. As a matter of course, any field representatives for your service business should be tasked with regularly chatting with the customers or clients to find out what the competition is doing.

Another route to understanding what your competitors offer is to utilize Freedom of Information Legislation for the jurisdiction(s) where you operate. Many times, companies you compete against will also provide services to government and a range of documents, from quotes and proposals through to final outputs, can often be obtained this way. This can give tremendous insight into the competition's work product, its appearance, its content, and other facets.

Another stratagem is to identify and speak with ex-employees of the competitors to learn as much as possible about what goes on behind closed doors, the presentations, meetings, telephone calls, lunches, and the like, which you can never see in the open yourself. Such employees should be cautioned not to divulge anything that is proprietary to their former employer or that might be considered confidential, but a general sense from them, as to what competitors are offering, can be invaluable.

What To Do With the CI You Gather

Once you have identified your competitors' services, teased them apart to learn what the components are and put them back into a continuum, as experienced by the clients, it is time to make use of the findings. If your own service offering is lacking in comparison, you can use your competitive intelligence to decide where and how you can improve. What do you need to add? Will it involve hiring? Adding external resources? Buying new equipment? If your competitors seem to have smoother execution from start to finish with each customer they service, how can you adapt to first mirror, then surpass them?

For the cases where you may be doing better, your CI will spotlight the weaknesses of competitors and show you where you need to build on your strengths in your marketing materials and in client presentations. But first, you may need to study your competitors' marketing initiatives; it may just be that their superior marketing is helping to sell an inferior service and you need to explore this issue as well.

Defining Their Service

- Try and obtain copies of traditional competitors' quotes or proposals. Routes to this include asking customers or ex-customers along with requests placed under the FOIA legislation for anything submitted to government.

- Speak to customers/clients on a regular basis or engage someone to do this for you, to learn exactly what traditional competitors are offering.

- Track alliances or other partnerships formed by your traditional competitors to see where they might be offering a value-added service.

- Monitor directory listings, ads, Yellow Pages, and more to see how competitors are describing what they do.

- Tap their ex-employees for nonproprietary insight about competitors' service offerings.

CHAPTER 11

The Marketing Challenge

So, you've found them, figured out where they want to go, and know what they're selling; the next challenge is to determine how your traditional competitors are marketing their services, because this will not only let you in on how successful they are but also provide you with a tool to re-examine and fine-tune your own marketing plan.

While it is true some service businesses advertise their services and otherwise describe themselves in the public domain, most services marketing is not visible to the naked eye. Services marketing tends to occur via proposals, quotes, sales presentations, and handshakes; in many lines of work, there are no ads in print media, on radio, or TV. People-to-people marketing is heavily used. Alternatively, a service business may rely exclusively on direct marketing, which uses mailing lists and databases, none of which can be readily examined. Brochures and other collateral material may be the media selected to get the message out. While it is true in more recent years that some service businesses have set up Web sites, which anyone can access, Internet-based marketing still represents the tip of the iceberg, leaving most services marketing hidden. And, for many firms, none of these are needed; there are, in this world, long-established firms that can rely solely on the oldest marketing strategy in existence: word-of-mouth.[1]

The Role of the Handshake

The obscurity of marketing in services came quickly to the surface when, a few years ago, a company in the telemarketing industry decided to learn more about its competitors, especially who they were and what they offered. At the time, telemarketing had something of a sleazy image, being associated with boiler-room selling, and so the industry did not have a very public face. Since then, of course, it has become much more sophisticated with the introduction of computer telephony integration and has a much cleaner image, although the inevitable telephone calls, which come during dinner, are still as frustrating as ever!

One of the first challenges in this case was identifying just who offered telemarketing. It is often true with services that there will be companies that provide the service on a stand-alone basis and those that offer the service as an ancillary service to some other activity. Some telemarketing companies were identified through space advertising in marketing industry publications while Yellow Pages listings turned up a few more. However, there was a suspicion that this did not represent the universe of providers involved, and so an extensive search began to trawl through directories, articles, and many other sources to identify the full range of companies active in this sector.

This stage of the research having been completed, a master list of companies was developed, but this was only a starting point. The next step involved obtaining literature from them—an activity complicated by the fact that not every telemarketing service had a brochure describing its services. Eventually, it became necessary to talk to account executives or senior managers at each of the companies to learn about the services they offered and glean hints of how these services were marketed. This quickly revealed that, at the time, many contracts for telemarketing services were awarded on a handshake basis between old friends. The role of influencers quickly became apparent; in many cases, an executive who had worked at an advertising agency had left to start a telemarketing business and so relied on referrals from friends at his old agency to obtain business. It was soon obvious that "who knows whom" was a major marketing strategy in this particular industry.

Direct Marketing and Selling

Not all service businesses can rely on a handshake, but many do rely on direct selling and use account executives. While it may be easy to identify the existence of such salespeople, it is much harder to find out what the reps do, their effectiveness, their chemistry with the client, how discussions pitching their services proceed, how they describe what they do, and the other elements of marketing activities. Learning about these issues via competitive intelligence can open an important window on how effectively or not your own business has kept pace with market shifts.

This was brought home to Inchcape Testing Services, as it was then known, when the firm was at a crossroads over renewing the lease on its textile testing laboratory in New York City. The lab had once done a roaring trade, but demand had dropped in the years leading up to the investigation. Perhaps Inchcape would be better to close the facility and amalgamate services with the nearby New Jersey location, the director of marketing mused. How had competitors fared in the same period? Had they also experienced a decline in demand?

Research was undertaken across a number of constituencies; the competitors were one, the customers—comprising fiber mills, yarn mills, textile mills, converters, garment manufacturers, retailers, and dry cleaners—were others. What the customers revealed was that there had been a shift; fiber and yarn mills and, to a lesser extent, textile mills and converters, had brought their testing in-house, often using technologies known as in-line testing. The bulk of demand for the services of a testing lab had shifted to the higher value-added segments of the chain: the manufacturers, retailers, and cleaners. Once the results were presented, the director of marketing summarized the findings this way: "What we have is not a market problem but a marketing problem."

Even more important was the discovery that competing labs had not been "asleep at the wheel" while market shifts had occurred. Their marketing efforts had been switched to the three segments of the value-added chain, which still needed outside support from a testing lab. Their literature had been redesigned and mailed out appropriately; when the competing labs were large enough to have account reps or field sales people, these individuals had been reorganized accordingly, with titles changed as necessary to reflect their new marketing focus.

Mail Pieces, Software, and More

If your competitors do direct marketing or database marketing, then they likely use brochures, newsletters, postcards, card packs, and other print pieces. Rather than wait until a crisis like the one facing Inchcape presents itself, it is better for any services firm to find ways to get on the mailing lists of competing organizations. This way, you'll have a ready indicator of when market shifts occur and how your competitors are responding to them. If it would be too obvious for your company to list itself, can you identify a substitute, such as a neighbor or perhaps use a home address, to slip past the net and put yourself in a position to receive their brochures, newsletters, and other marketing materials?

Another tool used nowadays in direct marketing or direct selling is the piece of software designed by a services firm and intended to intrigue the prospective client about the services available. Such software will often be developed to help the client solve or start to solve a problem: this can include developing a business plan, finding a new approach to inventory management, or identifying tactics for customer retention. Large management consulting firms, IT consulting firms, merchandising services companies, meeting planners, human resources and process consultants will all send out software, the idea being to tease the client and get him reaching for the phone to call the firm for more.

CD-ROMs can also be developed with this kind of marketing in mind, as can videos. These two items represent the electronic equivalent of the print brochure. While services should be selected on their intrinsic merits, even if yours is the better firm, you may be "left in the dust" by competitors who are using such slick tools, and so it is important to find out whether such packages exist.

Tracking Their Ads

Of course, if your competitors do advertise, you will want to set up a means of tracking these ads. Such advertisements will likely fall into two categories: image ads, which tend to be placed in high-profile business magazines or in trade publications for your own industry, and smaller classified ads, placed in the trade magazines read by the customers or clients.

Some service organizations make heavy use of such paid advertising—known as space advertising—with strong examples being American Express, many banks and financial institutions, large management consulting firms, computer or IT consulting firms, and the like. When looking for a competitor's ads, it's important to leave no stone unturned in your search. The most effective advertising usually rests on finding the less crowded avenues to reach customers. For this reason, your competitors may avoid your industry trade magazine and turn elsewhere. An ad agency catering to industrial accounts may avoid ad industry publications and even the more obvious manufacturing industry magazines and instead buy space in journals catering to accountants and financial officers, who just happen to work at its targets. Other options include buying ads in publications put out by charities and other nonprofits.

Event Marketing

Another very frequently used strategy for services marketing, notably by large management consulting firms, accounting firms, and law firms, is the seminar or conference, presented strictly for a group of clients. Just finding out about these events can be challenging, but if you have managed to infiltrate a competitor's mailing list or database, you should receive regular notices when such events are being held. These will often involve speakers, some sort of meal—events designed around lunches or breakfasts are common—and a program where consultants from the host service business represent most of the speakers. A guest speaker may be invited in to give the event less of a biased feel. Even if your competitors do not host their own events, they may make it a practice to speak regularly at a range of conferences and seminars, notably where such are for the client's or customer's industry rather than your own industry.

Another approach to event marketing used by services and goods-producers is the sponsorship of a major sporting or cultural event. This type of marketing is frequently used when a firm wants to reposition itself or market itself as a brand (see Chapter 9). Opera, ballet, and jazz festivals are just three types of cultural events where your competitors may be sponsors, while everything from horse races to stock car races,

gymnastics competitions to curling and hockey may attract a competing organization to pony up enough cash for marquee status. One of
the dangers in not finding this out via a CI initiative is the way such
activities can put your company at a perceptual disadvantage in the
eyes of customers or influencers, unless you implement measures to
counteract the impressions being created by your competitors.

Referral Marketing

A further marketing strategy that service businesses use is to belong
to associations that maintain databases and referral services. In fact, if
the referral service is strong, companies offering a particular service
may do no other form of marketing. This was discovered during research
into the merchandising services business discussed in Chapter 8. Similar to the telemarketing services industry example outlined earlier in
this chapter, merchandising services is not very high profile in how it
markets and advertises itself, relying instead on a lot of word-of-mouth,
repeat business, and referrals from an industry database. During the
investigation in question, one of the better sources identified was the
referral database of the National Association of Retail Merchandising
Services (NARMS). Although it may be a surprising suggestion, it is
common for a company to be in an industry and offering services and
still not know about such a gold mine for business generation. When
you are investigating your competitors, be sure you have not overlooked
the existence of such referral services. Even if they are unknown to you,
they may be well known to—and well used by—your competitors.

Rainmakers

The fact that a handshake may seal a deal or that a direct sales force
may bring in the business suggests that a people-only-based marketing approach may be the sole method used to promote a business in
the services sector.

The individuals who go out to drum up new business may have no
other duties but to wine and dine customers and prospective clients;
these employees or partners are often referred to as rainmakers. For

many years, legal firms relied more or less exclusively on this approach for marketing their services. Such individuals will often hold memberships in tony clubs and have the use of boxes at major sporting events to support their work. For this reason, it can pay off from an intelligence point of view to scan the society pages of the newspaper or other publications, to see which partners or principals at your competitors are out hobnobbing and with whom; this can reveal a major part of their marketing strategy to you, in full living color!

Word of Mouth

Then, there are the really puzzling traditional competitors, as discussed in Chapter 5: the firms that do no advertising, no longer have a brochure, never set up a Web site, and seem to have few, if any, rainmakers or people calling on prospective customers. Faced with such a competitor, it is easy to wonder: How on earth do they stay in business?

In such cases, the secret may lie in how long they've been operating and how well they do their work. These factors—combined with a certain uniqueness to their offering—may allow them to rely strictly on word-of-mouth for their marketing. This means customer satisfaction (discussed in Chapter 13) is the primary driver of their business, and your primary source of competition. When you encounter such competitors, it is important to determine how entrenched they are and how they got to this point, so you can understudy them and achieve the same position at some point.

The Role of Relationship Management

This suggests that truly understanding how traditional competitors market their services and how to best them in the marketplace relies on exploring the relationship they have with each and every client. Since this is a task of some magnitude, it needs to be broken down into manageable steps. Since most service businesses, particularly smaller businesses, do not have the manpower to get out and speak to all the clients and prospective clients in this fashion, a logical starting point is to focus on prospective clients who have asked for a proposal, or had you in for a sales presentation, but have not bought, and try to determine *why* your company was not selected and why they chose the supplier they did select. Was it the other guy's brochure? His or her presentation? What swayed the decision? As often as not, it will turn out that the prior relationship had a lot to do with the supplier selection. (This raises another concern for the service business: being asked to quote to meet the client company's requirements of obtaining three quotes before making a decision. In cases where you are "always the bridesmaid, never the bride," an equally important part of your competitive intelligence is to notice this pattern and perhaps elect in future not to put in a bid. It may save you time and money in the long run and free you up to concentrate on more profitable prospects, those companies that will actually buy from you.)

In the cases where the prior relationship has been pivotal in the decision, you can then isolate the particular competitor and start to determine how they do their marketing. Do they use newsletters? Do they host events for clients, such as lunches or seminars? What marketing-related activities cement the relationship? Equally, you need to study the customer/influencer side of the equation, to determine how to swing this in your favor.

In such a climate, it is easy to see the value of the influencer database built by National Fuel Gas, discussed in Chapter 3. By learning not only who the influencers in its territory were but also the relationships between them, National Fuel was much better positioned to take control of its markets. Any messages sent to influencers, such as brochures, could convey a consistent message across all groups that were connected while, for any seminars or focus groups the company held, consultants who worked together could be invited to the same event. This allowed for a much greater level of reinforcement of the marketing messages National Fuel had to get across.

Yet another avenue to explore are relationships of long standing that come into play at both the decision-maker and the influencer level. Information about these relationships can be determined by looking at *Who's Who* type directories, studying alumni periodicals from colleges, determining club memberships, investigating ethnic affiliations, such as belonging to bicameral chambers of commerce, and otherwise determining who knows whom. If you compete against service businesses that are publicly traded, it is worthwhile to find out who is on the Board of Directors and explore this avenue. Such directors are usually listed in the annual reports, which can be obtained for free.

Segmentation Strategies

It can be equally difficult to probe marketing at a broader level and to determine how a service business segments its market, whether it does so by demographics, by geography, by size of account, or by some other variable. Even worse, there is always the risk that, with any public-domain manifestations of marketing strategy, there is a bit of "smoke and mirrors" in that the public face of the marketing campaign may be deliberately skewed to throw competitors off track while the real positioning of the service is only seen by clients and prospective customers.

It is not a given that two traditional competitors segment the same market the same way. This is illustrated in how banks segment and serve their markets. For example, the seniors market may, for some institutions, describe customers aged 50 and up, while others segment at 65 years and beyond and cater their services accordingly. Similarly, "small business" may be a segment with revenues up to $10 million or it may encompass businesses up to $50 million, depending on the size of the overall market. Alternatively, some banks use employee numbers to separate their small business markets from the next tier up, which may be known as the mid-market segment. The breaks for separation between small and mid-market may be as low as 50 employees or as high as 150.

While these divisions into segments may seem like arbitrary playing with numbers and the whole exercise somewhat academic, knowing about and analyzing a competitor's segmentation strategy can be extremely important: their market segments may be a better choice and help them make more money than you!

Where to Look for Intelligence About Marketing

An all-out effort to place your company or yourself on your competitors' mailing lists or in their database—if they use e-mail for marketing—should at least lay the foundations of good competitive intelligence about marketing. But such a tactic will not yield all the information you need.

Regular scanning for ads, articles, photographs, looking at any Web sites your competitors have, checking up on sponsors of events, and noting any toll-free numbers they are using are all important parts of the mix. If yours is a business where quotes or proposals are regularly used, you can ask your competitors' former customers if they are willing to share; this is usually best done during an in-person visit, as opposed to phone or e-mail. Or, if your competitors bid on government work, place Freedom of Information requests to obtain copies of proposals submitted. Once any tender or bid is closed and the supplier has been chosen, such documents should be available.

Networking with customers and suppliers may also be an effective route to gathering intelligence about competitors' marketing initiatives; suppliers may include the printers, designers, and others who contribute to marketing materials while customers are on the receiving end. Clients can also be a source of intelligence about special events, such as seminars, which your competitors are using.

Then there are trade shows and exhibits; if these are actively used for marketing by firms in your particular services sector, you need to be aware not only of events at which you and your competitors exhibit but also of those where you do not participate but your competitors do.

What To Do With the CI You Gather

The intelligence you gather about competitors' marketing activities can be used not only to understand what they're doing but also to improve what you're doing to increase your success. Perhaps their collateral material, such as their brochure, is couched in more customer-friendly terms? Perhaps they explain the benefits of the services you both offer better than you do? It is always possible to study what they've done and go one better to improve your own materials.

You can also use intelligence about competitors' marketing to spot what they've forgotten and seize opportunities. This can include overlooked or underserved segments and untapped markets. The traditional competitors may not be doing the best job on relationship management with their customers, and your marketing CI may reveal their weak spots; they may not have a newsletter, for example, but you will be in a position to introduce one—or improve what you already have—to take advantage of the situation. Of course, the most comprehensive marketing strategy will be of no use to your competitors if, once they have landed the business, they fall down on the job. In learning where their strengths and weaknesses lie, you need to look closely at how they deliver, if they can at all, which is examined in Chapter 12.

References

"Promoting the Professions." *Business Quarterly*. Summer 1997: 64-70.

Understanding Marketing

- When proposals and quotes are heavily used in your sector, tap customers/clients or file FOIA requests with the government to obtain copies of your competitors' efforts.

- Find ways to get on their mailing lists so you regularly receive newsletters or brochures.

- Place yourself on a wide range of other mailing lists to learn about marketing tactics as diverse as card packs or seminar speaking.

- Attend events where your competitors are speaking or exhibiting, plus track sponsorship of athletic, cultural, and other events.

- Check *Who's Who*, alumni, and other directories along with annual reports to learn about relationships your traditional competitors use in their marketing efforts.

CHAPTER 12

Can They Deliver?

Much of the content of this book has focused on some of the inherent difficulties in gathering intelligence in service businesses; one of the further disadvantages of investigating services is that your traditional competitors don't necessarily display how they get from A to B in providing their services. As Michael Porter's definition illustrates, providers may go to the customer's site to perform their service or the customer may come in to the competitor's site. Or, they may use other distribution channels including couriers, electronic delivery, or the phone, which are not easy to study; the effectiveness of such channels, however, and the timeliness of the competition's delivery are no less important for services businesses to investigate than they are for goods-producing businesses. Delivery is also important as an area for investigation because it may invoke the input of influencers as a form of competition as well as generate customer-origin competition; all the more reason to include it on your radar screen. Beyond such physical delivery issues, there is also that of psychological delivery; can the competing firm come through in terms of their advice and its quality? And how valid is this work over time?

Customer Site Delivery

Services will often be delivered on-site at the customer's or client's premises. This can be true of as diverse a range of services as accounting, business brokerage, security services, executive recruitment, insurance, equipment repair or servicing, and various forms of management consulting.

The following example illustrates why such customer-site delivery complicates the study of this aspect of a traditional competitor's activities. A provider of natural gas services, facing slowing growth in its traditional markets (which were constrained by geographical service territory boundaries), was looking to expand into value-added services and settled on the idea of energy audits. Such energy audits would be offered to homeowners to enable them to assess ways they could stabilize or reduce their energy bills, a particularly valuable service in climates with high heating or cooling bills. The gas company had no idea if any of its traditional competitors, such as the hydroelectric distribution companies, were offering energy audits, nor did they have a sense of how many independent providers there might be in the marketplace. Other questions naturally came to the surface: How were the audits being delivered? How were they being priced? Were they even being sold or were they offered for free? What were the coverages of those providing such services, in terms of geography and types of home served? Since the gas company could not easily explore these issues directly, it contracted with an independent company to investigate.

It quickly became apparent, once work began, that the only real way to understand how most energy audit services were being delivered was to actually experience them. Normally, the range of services being offered in any given sector can be determined from Yellow Pages phone books and other directories, both print and online, but, as discussed in Chapter 8, some sectors are hidden. In this case, few if any providers were listed in conventional sources. It took phone calls to likely suspects and networking with industry contacts to create a list of candidate suppliers. Once the potential suppliers had been identified, more data was gathered about their delivery methods. What then transpired is that some audit services sent out a questionnaire by mail while other providers came out to the home to work on site. This meant mail-out questionnaires were requested while staff members at the research company undertaking the study volunteered their homes and proceeded to receive providers of these audit services over a period of several days. Had they not pursued this step, the research company would have had no idea about the caliber of personnel sent out on the audit by each of the selected firms, the depth of the service they provided, the ability of the service provider to customize the service to the individual home in question (e.g., existing heating methods; age and construction materials of home; homeowner's budget for any upgrades required; etc.), promptness of service delivery (e.g., did the energy audit provider show up on time as agreed?) and similar facets of service delivery. Similarly, for the mail-out questionnaires, their timeliness of arrival, whether they came express or regular mail, and such data had to be noted.

This example suggests that delivery in a service business can be more multifaceted than it is in a goods-producing business. In a goods-producing industry, it is obviously important that the right parts and the right number of them are in the box and that they are packaged properly, shipped promptly, and arrive at the correct destination. But once received, it is fairly easy for the customer to check whether the order is correct or not and specify exactly what is wrong, if any corrective action is needed. In contrast, checking that a service—such as a competitor's service—has been fully delivered is not a quick task. And comparisons between services are also difficult to make. For the energy audits, charts had to be prepared to make meaningful comparisons between the mail-in options and the services provided on-site.

Provider Site Delivery

Sectors where the customer or client comes in to the service provider's premises include law, banking, and services in the medical field, such as massage therapy or dentistry; this may also be an option for computer and equipment repair and naturally covers a whole range of personal services such as hairstyling and manicures.

To return to the private banking example used in Chapter 11, there can be a tremendous range of customer experiences just within the confines of one private banking location. Whether or not the customer likes the location, the atmosphere, the decor, the hours of operation and more, can have a strong bearing on the customer's decision to remain with this particular bank or switch to another supplier. Such customer defections can therefore be triggered by the mode of delivery, long before the core financial services have been provided.

When your competitors do have multiple locations, you may be able to examine how consistent delivery is from site to site. Whatever its shortcomings in other areas, Lasik Vision (Chapter 6) had achieved a great deal of uniformity between all its locations, from the appearance of its lobbies on up to how procedures were performed. This meant a customer who had vision correction in one location for one eye would encounter a great deal of similarity in delivery if he happened to stop off, in a completely different city, to get the other eye corrected or needed some follow-up work done.

Another reason to keep tabs on both customer-site and provider-site delivery is to track when there has been a switch. Back in the early days of the personal computer industry, technicians invariably visited the customer's site to perform service, but as the industry matured, a carry-in option became available. This had an impact on pricing for services and allowed firms offering the carry-in option to be even more competitive on price.

Third Party Site Delivery

Luckily, for some services sectors, delivery by competing organizations occurs at a third party's site, which does afford the opportunity to study the competition's execution and delivery at close quarters. This can include the work of meeting and event planners (hotels, conference centers, convention centers), consulting engineers (buildings and infrastructures), lawyers (courts), architects, interior designers and decorators (offices, hotels, restaurants), and landscapers (industrial parks and public gardens).

While the third party site will only allow you to assess the visible elements of delivery, it does provide some intelligence to use as a base for further investigation. With meetings, are the attendees satisfied or are they milling about the lobby, grumbling? Is signage to the meeting clear? Did any planned meal service arrive on time? These and similar questions can be answered by a visit to the third party site during the event. Chatting with the staff of the third party, such as hotel employees, may also yield some valuable insights.

Some of the examples already cited, such as the merchandising services case, illustrate how third party site delivery allows more detailed investigation of how a competitor delivers. A company in this sector, having identified which merchandisers maintain the racks at which retailers, can always go to those stores and see how well the individuals are performing their work or even observe them on the job.

In the case of the IVR industry, the personals business discussed in Chapter 8, the use of Web sites as a prime delivery channel allows any company wishing to study this aspect of its traditional competitors' delivery an open window to do so.

By Mail, Fax, or Modem

Another frequent option, especially if a report is the deliverable, is to mail or courier the result of the service to the customer or client's premises. This is true of many research services, management consulting services, financial and investment analyses, travel arrangements, and more. A common practice is to marry this delivery of a hard copy item with an on-site presentation to explain the results to the client. In recent years, electronic delivery via modem has also been increasingly used by services businesses that have a deliverable fitting this mode of distribution. Financial services is one example, as is the research industry.

Consider how the increasing use of electronic distribution in banking has created new challenges for financial institutions wishing to study their traditional competitors. As well as the physical element—the ATM itself, its location, its dimensions, how well lit it is—there is the issue of software and how user-friendly or otherwise this is, the reliability of systems (is delivery reliable or do systems crash frequently?), and level of frustration or otherwise experienced by the customer in using the ATM. This is all in addition to studying what is being delivered over the ATM; plain vanilla transaction banking services or more sophisticated, value-added offerings, such as investments or insurance?

Over the Phone

It is equally possible, in services, to deliver over the phone, with no physical contact between services provider and client. This has long been the practice in services sectors such as stockbrokering; clients phone in for quotes and the broker phones back with the answer. The fact that such transactions may now occur via e-mail is somewhat academic; whether by phone or e-mail, such a delivery practice is hard to observe if you are a company intent on studying the competition. Foreign exchange services are a further example of a phone-dependent business (although there has been some migration to the Internet) while lawyers have long dispensed advice to clients by phone.

Do They Go On Delivering?

Initial delivery of the service is one thing; some consideration of how the advice stands up over time is important. In the area of legal services, for example, the lawyer's advice at the time it is given, such as for an acquisition or the divestiture of part of a client's business, might seem very solid, but how the advice weathers the test of time, whether or not there are tax implications arising at a later date, which are troublesome for the client, whether the client finds themselves entangled in other legal issues arising from the original advice, mean that the effectiveness of the legal service is not a one-time and one-time-only event but is revealed over a continuum. The willingness or availability of the advisor to step forward at a later date, especially when a situation sours, can be another distinguishing characteristic of services delivery.

Tracking how a competitor's advice or service stands the test of time can be crucial in identifying when there is a bad apple in your industry sector, spoiling things for everybody else. This is another example of where, in service businesses, customer-origin competition along with influencer competition come into play. Bad experiences occurring to customers or clients and their influencers (and their memories of the same) can prove a much greater competitive threat over the years than the specific actions of the traditional competitor who gives the bad advice; it may well be that the traditional competitor goes out of business and is no longer a presence in the marketplace, whereas the bad taste left in everyone's mouth lingers as a competitive threat for many, many years.

This is why a key part of competitive intelligence for an established supplier is to keep tabs on new market entrants, the segment of providers that is newly formed but promising to become traditional competition. If a new entrant is still "green," they may make life difficult for others in the industry by poor execution and delivery. If they fail to deliver on time, they may seriously damage the interests of a customer who may then prove a hard sell for all manner of service providers.

The newcomer may engineer this unfortunate set of circumstances because they have previously worked in a large company with a lot of support and resources and may have underestimated what would be required to get the job done. Or, they may have low-balled their bid to land a piece of business and then found they cannot complete the work within budget. Whatever the reason for the failed delivery, it is a competitive threat that needs monitoring as part of your intelligence initiative.

Knowing about your traditional competitor's people—explored in-depth in Chapter 15—becomes essential under these circumstances. If the staff at a competing services firm are responsible for execution and delivery, then their personal resources—their track records, reputation and the like—will have a bearing on how well your competitors, as entities, can deliver.

Where to Look for Intelligence About Delivery

What are some of the tactics a service business can use to track its competitors' delivery and determine how the delivery of their service does or doesn't constitute a competitive threat? Obviously, one of the best ways with provider-site delivery is to find some way to experience the competitor's service, as occurred with the energy audit services. In the case of a national competitor, with many branches or distributorships, it is possible to do this yourself, on an anonymous basis. Take, for example, a tax preparation service like H&R Block. If you, yourself, are in the business of providing tax preparation services, either as a stand-alone service or part of a package of accounting services, it is perfectly possible to go and experience the H&R Block service if there is an office in your town, because you will not be dealing with the principals of the company and there are certain standardized aspects of the service that will be common to all the company's locations. However, if you offer a local service and compete simply against local providers who may know you very well and recognize your face, you may have to resort to paying someone else to experience competitive services.

Third party site delivery probably offers the widest scope for tracking by a competitor. With the case of merchandising services, as suggested, it is possible to go to retail stores and see these firms in action. Services your competitors provide at hotels or convention centers (seminars, meetings, conferences and the like) are also open to both observation and experience. Any delivery that occurs over an open channel like the Web also lends itself to ready study.

Probably the hardest to study, unless you yourself become a client, is delivery at the customer's site. This is why, to explore this type of delivery, and gather meaningful intelligence, you will either have to engage the services of a mystery shopping service or network with mutual customers of you and your competitors to obtain useful data.

What To Do With the CI You Gather

When it comes to the physical delivery aspects of your competitors' activities, you need to assess how you may or may not be at a competitive advantage or disadvantage on account of what they are doing. If they go to the customer's site while you insist the customer comes to your premises, they may be seen as more flexible while enjoying lower overhead costs when your experience is the reverse.

Electronic delivery methods, once you have intelligence showing competitors are using fax, modem, or e-mail, may also create a further cost advantage for them or be perceived as being more customer-friendly. All these discoveries provide pointers and suggestions for modifying your own business.

How your competitors are faring in psychological delivery can also offer you points of leverage to develop competitive advantage. If they are failing to deliver on time, or are not around to support their advice in later years, then your organization may gain a reputation for more reliability than competing firms in your industry.

Investigating Delivery

- Speak to customers or ex-customers of your traditional competitors to learn about delivery.

- Although mystery shopping services are mostly used in the goods-producing sectors, they can also be tapped to investigate delivery for services.

- Identify any user groups or chat rooms on the Web where your traditional competitors' customers or clients may share their delivery experiences.

- When possible, experience a traditional competitor's service directly.

- Keep tabs on new market entrants to see if they are coming through for the clients or if they are otherwise dropping the ball and earning your industry a bad name.

CHAPTER 13

Are They Different and Better?

In service businesses, customer service is not an afterthought; in most cases, it is the *raison d'être* of the business. And survival and profitability of the enterprise often hinge not only on how well customers are served, but on how customers *perceive* the service they receive. Knowing how your traditional competitors are serving their customers and what they are doing to set themselves apart is key; how this service spills over to affect other forms of competition, such as influencer competition, can be studied to find ways to increase the growth of your own business. What is the scope of competitors' service? Do they confine their service to traditional 9–5 business hours or have they moved to 24/7? In a nutshell, are your traditional competitors really different and better? And, if they are, what can you do about it to compete more effectively?

The Elements of Service

Prior to gathering intelligence to determine how service sets your competitors apart, it is useful to identify what the elements of "different and better" service might be. Another way of looking at the issue is to turn it around and approach it from the angle of customer satisfaction. Some facets of this—such as delivery, the ability to meet deadlines, or to offer quick turnaround—have been covered in Chapter 12. But these elements of service might be considered basic; in doing what they do to be different and better, your traditional competitors likely go considerably beyond timeliness or punctuality. Instead, they are

153

likely striving for what's known as "knock your socks off" service and looking for ways to surprise and delight their customers or clients. This can encompass a whole mix of issues: from courtesy—recognizing the customer and calling them by name when they phone in—on up through anticipating: knowing that a customer or client has an unexpressed or future need and delivering on it today.

Service can also encompass the ease of use of locations where services are performed, hours of access, waiting times—whether on the phone or in person—and customer comfort while waiting, to the completeness of the service, the little extras included: Is fresh coffee always waiting when a customer shows up at your competitor's location? Do all your clients competitors' receive roses or chocolates on Valentine's Day? Plus, how are problems and complaints resolved? To this aspect of service, you can also add the issue of retention rates, the number or percentage of your competitors' clients or customers who continue to do business with them. There is probably no greater indication that, in some way, however hard to detect, a firm is different and better than in the percentage of its repeat business.

How Available Are They?

A starting point for this service differentiation may well hinge on how available your competitors are compared to you. Do they work from one location or from multiple locations? For example, some airlines have one call center operating 24/7 to handle customer questions and otherwise provide service. Yet other airlines will have distributed call centers where calls are relayed to the next available operator who may be in another part of the country from the customer calling. The relayed method may offer more instantaneous response to customer calls and greater customer satisfaction. Or, it may frustrate customers who prefer to deal with someone locally. This is why service and customer satisfaction need to be examined together.

In the case of professional services, management consulting firms, such as the Big Five, have offices throughout the country and may even have three or four offices in the same city. Yet other management consulting firms will have but one location serving clients nationwide. If you compete against such firms, you need to identify where all their locations are (an issue touched on in Chapter 8) what services are offered from each, how they operate to avoid cannibalizing business from each other (in the case of multiple locations) or, in the case of a one-location operation, how effectively they can serve clients outside their geographic territory or if they even do. Again, such investigations, to provide a valuable tool, need to be married to customer and influencer intelligence gathering to truly understand how these two groups perceive the service they receive.

Just How Good Are They?

One of the difficulties in finding out about customer satisfaction is that services are so frequently delivered one-to-one that observing them is next to impossible, and any intelligence may have to rest on second and third party reports. Then, the subtle differences among all these one-to-one experiences will take time to collect, sort, and analyze.

For example, if you are in the temporary help services business and want to find out about your competitors' service, once you have identified who your traditional competitors are, you will have to explore two dimensions of what each does. On the one hand, there is the interaction between each temporary help agency and the client company requesting their services, and then there is the interaction between the temporary worker placed on site, at the client's, and the client. This means that company investigating its competitors in this industry needs to learn about selection procedures and competency tests that the competing agency uses to select and rank employees before they are placed at client sites, the way each agency interacts with its clients, how they follow up once the placement has occurred, what sorts of guarantees they give, how quickly they move to replace someone who is not working out, how they respond to real crises and problems, and so on. Some of the these procedures will be standard for all their clients while others, such as acting to address problems or replace someone who is not working out, will be more individualized.

Then, of course, there is the actual experience of the company on the receiving end that has contracted with the temp agency, and what they go through when they have the temporary on the job. Did the temp go the "extra mile?" Or was the person someone with attitude? Customer satisfaction levels need to be investigated to determine how effective service really is. For a placement agency, different and better may mean a higher level of successful first time placements and fewer recalls than others in the industry. This is another case where customer and influencer competition intersects with provider competition; all need to be studied.

Or, to return to the private banking services referenced in other chapters, for one bank to determine the service levels at another bank and customer satisfaction requires ongoing investigation tapping multiple sources. First, the investigating bank has to find out about the setting for service performance: where the private banking offices of the competitor are, how luxurious these offices are, how spacious, what the feel of the place is when the clients walk in, and more. Then, the investigating bank needs to find out something about the interaction that occurs between the consultant and the client once they have entered the consultant's private office and closed the door. In this, there is probably no one single way that a consultant will interact with a client but the performance of the service will be tailored to each customer, meaning there is no pattern. There may, however, be industry norms or standards that the consultant has to follow, which will probably be the only way to establish an initial benchmark. Then, there is the issue of reporting back to the client; the ease of use of the reports or their complexity is just one dimension. Then the financial institution making the investigation will have to look beyond the obvious to determine if other services, such as concierge-type services, are provided to private banking clients, by the competitor, as a perk. This might include obtaining theater tickets for a client from out of town or agreeing to mail the client's bills while the client is on holiday. Again, such services are not standard from client-to-client but will be tailored to each one, according to need; for each competitor, you need to ask: how are they different and better?

Knowing that both customers and competitors would be comparing its services to others in the marketplace was what led Investore, the Bank of Montreal's money management service, to take steps to differentiate its services from those of the competition. One way the bank did this was to be proactive and provide customers with information, comparing Investore to the competition. When customers went into a retail outlet, literature awaited them giving such details. Another way was to offer a service for children, called the "My Money Investment Club," something the competition wasn't doing. Then there was the Investore Mobile, which went to outlying areas to provide services.[1] Such initiatives all worked together to try to communicate that Investore was different and better, beginning with convenient locations in high traffic retail malls and ending with the "don't come to us, we'll come to you" service of the mobile.

Do They Measure Customer Satisfaction?

Even when your competitors strive to "knock the customers' socks off," they may not just assume they did okay but undertake formal measurement of customer satisfaction. Part of any intelligence gathering campaign to probe service should try to determine if there is such a formal customer satisfaction measurement initiative or whether the matter is attacked on an ad hoc basis, as and when time permits. Note that the presence of the former does not mean that your competitors have greater customer retention than the latter; sometimes, clients can be surveyed to death about how well their suppliers are doing and the whole program becomes counter-productive. When gathering intelligence about service, always be prepared to filter your findings through the prism of what works and what doesn't.

In cases where there are formal surveys, how often are these used? Are they sent out quarterly to every client regardless of whether they have used the service? Or are such surveys simply sent out on a project-by-project basis, once the work is completed? What is the return rate? Then, you will need to look at the reaction and turnaround on resolving any complaints along with who gets involved. If a customer of one of your services competitors has complained, does the competitor resolve this by using the same people who worked on the original piece of work or do higher level people at the firm step in? How many of such complaint situations are resolved to the customer's satisfaction? One way to find out answers to these questions is to become a customer of your competitors—if this is possible—and participate firsthand in their satisfaction measurement process.

If direct participation isn't an option, then an alternate route to the intelligence is to conduct your own satisfaction survey and ask mutual customers how your follow-up compares to the competition's. This was the stratagem used a few years ago by Royal Trust during a survey of its security cage service customers. (The use of cages predates the introduction of the Book-Based System now in use). Securities cages were used by financial institutions to complete trades and move securities back and forth. It was very much a person-to-person service, which further pitted competitors one against the other because each financial institution was automatically both a rival to and a customer of the other institutions.

Royal Trust knew it had a problem; it had lost business, and competitors were fully exposed to the inadequacies of the company's services. For two years in a row, Royal Trust conducted its own surveys to not only learn how its customers (rivals) felt about its services, but to learn how they were doing with their own service and its measurement. The survey the first year indicated that there was plenty of room for improvement but, by the second year, satisfaction toward Royal Trust was up and there were fewer complaints. Even better, the company learned that customer retention and customer satisfaction had slipped as far as perceptions of its rivals (customers) were concerned. The survey therefore turned into a dual tool: gathering CI while measuring customer satisfaction.

How Do They Handle Complaints?

As already touched on, complaint resolution is key to maintaining customer satisfaction levels; finding out how your competitors resolve complaints will be equally as challenging as finding out about how well they serve customers in the first place.

The variations possible in complaint resolution practices were discovered during an investigation undertaken by INX International Ink Company. Although the core product of this company is ink, the nature of the business nowadays is much more a service: technological advice, software, and around-the-clock live support for emergencies are all part of the "package" sold to large printers and packagers nationwide. INX wanted to know how other industries, some ink companies, and some providers of other services were handling complaints and how they were *using* this information to make their businesses different and better.

What the intelligence gathering exercise uncovered were approaches from very basic to highly sophisticated. And the more sophisticated a company's complaint resolution and utilization procedures were, the more willing the competitors to call a complaint or problem by name; the less sophisticated companies skirted the issue by asking their clients for feedback. INX also discovered competitors were using several tools to effect problem resolution: toll-free phone or fax numbers, complaint solicitation materials included with shipments to encourage calls about problems, proactive follow-up by technical experts to resolve service issues even before the customer called in about them and more. All these initiatives led to a high level of customer satisfaction and thus retention.

Going a step beyond this, your competitors may have a formal program to go after defecting customers or lost accounts. Another hallmark of the companies perceived as different and better during the INX investigation was the effort they devoted to finding out why a client did not renew with them or had suddenly stopped doing business. Such lost account action further increased perceptions about their commitment to service among the customers.

Involving the Customers in Service Differentiation

In a similar vein, it is always worthwhile to probe for the existence of customer or client councils at each competitor. By introducing key customers or clients into the "inner circle," such companies reinforce their commitment to service and also gain a source of ready customer feedback. This might be yet another form of competition your firm is up against. The existence of such an elect client group is an important discovery for another reason; it is likely that with such customers your competitors will pilot or test new services they are planning to introduce. Keeping tabs on such customers therefore also offers an avenue to learning about higher value-added or more integrated services that you will soon be facing in the marketplace.

Where to Look for Intelligence About Service Levels

How can a service business go about investigating and studying traditional competitors' service and its twin, customer satisfaction? There are different strategies available depending on the kind of service you offer. If you offer a service where you are not readily identified with your own business so that no one would recognize you or your staff, then it may be possible to learn first hand by actually experiencing the service. For example, a company offering car wash services would be able to regularly take vehicles to other competing car washes and experience the service first hand. In a similar fashion, the Red Lobster chain of restaurants, on an ongoing basis, pays for its employees to eat at competing restaurants so they will study the competition and find ways to improve Red Lobster's own service levels.

These strategies, however, may not work if you are high profile in your industry sector or if the intent of your visits to a competitor would be too obvious. For example, a lawyer who wanted to determine how competing legal firms prepare wills may have difficulty going in person to each and every competitor firm to have a will drawn up. This is a case where paying someone else to experience the service and report back on what they found may be the route to some useful intelligence. Such "mystery shopping" is a time-honored practice in retail, and there is no reason it cannot be effective in services. Many service businesses fall into this category of needing an intermediary to probe service; the head of a prominent ad agency cannot go to competing ad agencies and pretend he has a piece of business to place. Instead, speaking to the other agencies' clients on a regular basis and determining how they are finding the competing service is the way to learn about service levels. One of the triggers to determining which clients to speak with in the ad agency business can come when it is advertised in the trade press that the account is up for review. Similar "windows" to gathering intelligence will open up, from time to time, in other services sectors as well.

Another way to gauge the service level offered by competing companies is to see what they promise in their ads and brochures. Are there any stated objectives? If the service is, for example, tied to emergency interventions, what is the response rate promised? If your competitors have any kind of 800 or toll-free number to support their service levels, what can you learn by phoning up and asking some basic questions?

What To Do With the CI You Gather

Once you have pieced together an understanding of your competitors' service levels—how customers perceive them, what they have done to set themselves apart, how they measure customer satisfaction or deal with complaints, how they involve customers to achieve improvements, their availability—you need to scrutinize your own company against these variables and see how you measure up. Any areas where you are stronger than your competitors should be noted so you can maintain performance levels, while any weak spots can be addressed in light of your new learning.

References

"Investore." Ivey Management Services. 1999.

Scoping Out Service and Satisfaction

- Speak to customers or ex-customers of your traditional competitors to learn about customer/client satisfaction.

- Identify any user groups or chat rooms on the Web where your traditional competitors' customers or clients may share their experiences with service levels.

- Keep tabs on new market entrants to see if they are coming through for the clients or if they are otherwise "dropping the ball" and earning your industry a bad name.

- Determine if there is a customer or client council; speak with its representatives regularly.

- Call up any toll-free numbers to see what extras your traditional competitors are offering.

CHAPTER 14

All About Money

Any service firm investigating its competitors in the manner suggested so far in this book will have been able to learn a certain amount about such companies' activities from public-domain sources. Add to this observation—for example, when you meet representatives of competing firms at professional get-togethers or conference exhibits—and you will soon have a fairly good picture of them. One topic, however, will tend to remain private and require a good deal of sleuthing to uncover: How are they doing financially?

This may be one area where you will never know as an absolute how much a competing firm is making, but if you investigate their prices, costs, and sales or revenues, you may begin to move toward knowing this aspect of them. You can also get to know their marketing or delivery capabilities. Probably the most important thing to remember, when investigating money issues, is that *ranges* are often all you will be able to obtain. Once you have a range, it is always possible, over time, to refine this and narrow the spread.

Tackling the Pricing Challenge

In studying financial aspects of service businesses, the real *bête noir* of competitive intelligence is pricing. Whereas with products there are often what are known as "sticker prices" or "shelf prices" or "manufacturer's suggested retail price," there is rarely such an option with services. More than other aspects of competitive intelligence work, gathering pricing data is like completing a jigsaw puzzle; it takes time to put the pieces together. But probing this aspect of your competitor's services is also an important conduit to understanding other dimensions of service competition, namely, customers and influencers. Whatever the impact of these two competitive forces on your markets, no greater role for them will be found than in the arena of pricing. How customer and influencers *perceive* pricing—and the *value* of what is delivered—has a major impact on demand for your services and their willingness to buy from you, or any other supplier for that matter.

For Fee or For Free?

Sometimes, an investigation of pricing may turn up that some competitors or providers are supplying their services for free. This was one of the discoveries in the investigation into home energy audit services referenced in Chapter 12. At one end of the spectrum were private organizations, such as those run by contractors, who charged a fee to come out and analyze the home, the load factors, and make recommendations about energy savings; at the other end of the spectrum were the energy providers themselves, such as the hydro companies, which considered that supplying energy audit services was part of the overall package they offered to consumers. This meant that these firms rarely ever charged for audits. In terms of demand-side management, the utilities considered that finding ways for consumers to save energy actually helped them manage their supply/demand issues. This was a further reason they did not wish to charge for home energy audits. Discovering that there are competitive services that are not actually charging for a service you wish to offer on a fee basis further complicates the whole issue of competition in services. But it is an important discovery to make so you can find ways to compete against it effectively in the marketplace; the existence of free competition is often overlooked by new firms or established services entering new markets.

The role of government as a form of competition, discussed in Chapter 4, also comes to mind in the fee-versus-free debate. Many of the services offered through organizations such as UNICOR or CORCAN, using convict labor and not paying market wages as they do, can be marketed with very aggressive pricing or performed at-cost.

Another thorny issue for the service provider to probe and understand is the situation where the pricing being offered by competitors doesn't make sense and the service seems to be given away. In such cases, a competitor may be trying to "buy the business." This was the concern of a manufacturer of intraocular lenses, which are used in patients after cataract surgery. Since such lenses have to be inserted by ophthalmic surgeons, the pricing issue did not just hinge on what other makers of such intraocular lenses were charging for the product but also on the surgeons performing the procedure, their pricing, and how they went about doing their business. At issue was a discrepancy between what the lenses cost and the surgeons could charge for the procedure (this was in British Columbia where surgeons' fees, at the time, were capped) and what they seemed to be earning in contrast to these restrictions. There seemed to be some sort of kickback going on, from competing manufacturers to the surgeons, over and above any rebates offered. Such financial incentives were also handled in such a way that, from the surgeons' perspectives, the financial remuneration bypassed their books. It was only by gathering detailed intelligence from the surgeons that the manufacturer, put at a disadvantage, was able to address the practice and salvage its market share.

By the Hour or the Job?

How competitors quote on jobs may also need exploration. A time-honored practice in many service businesses has been to price by the hour; as discussed in Chapter 1, this is the basic unit of inventory in services, with varying degrees of value-add, which raise the price of the hour up or down. Legal firms, large accounting firms, and some management consulting firms still quote by the hour. But this practice is no longer as ubiquitous in service firms as it once was, even in firms that are more traditional and tend to charge that way. Quoting work by the job has become more widespread, especially as this allows many service firms to bury their per-hour rate. Market research, fee-based executive search, design services, consulting engineering, and others are more likely to quote by the job. Somewhere in between comes the practice of quoting per diem: research firms may do this, surveyors might, and some consulting engineering firms or management consulting firms will quote this way. There are also services sectors that set their fees as a percentage of the deal. This is true for mergers and acquisitions (M&A) specialists, business brokers and lawyers who handle class action or personal injury lawsuits.

All of which means, for someone gathering intelligence, that you need to not only gather raw dollar data but also determine the *basis* for the quote. It may also be true, depending on the size of the job, that one or more of your traditional competitors may quote lower rates as the size of the job or the number of hours involved increases; a commitment from a client to buy a large block of time usually gives the client some leverage, and so a sliding scale will come into effect.

Bundling and Packaging

Learning about a competitor's pricing is crucial when there is bundling of services. This is often the case in the financial services sector with large pension funds, investment management services, and private banking. One of the ways financial services institutions make their services palatable to their clients is to group them together; an organization, for example, which uses a bank for its pension fund management may get very favorable pricing if it also runs its payroll through the bank's services. Likewise, individuals who place all of their investments with one institution are often offered preferential pricing for their mortgages or car loans over those people who like to spread their money around. Then, many financial institutions, with their investment clients, will offer different interest rates for predetermined tiers of investments; the greater the dollars invested, the higher the interest rate. While this does not seem like a pricing issue, it is actually an aspect because it has a bearing on the client or customer's decision to place their funds with a particular institution.

Segmenting and Pricing

Providers of services can also resort to tactics that make it difficult for a competitor to understand their pricing or make meaningful comparisons. In the insurance business, for example, most services in life, health, and disability are sold on the basis of "size-bands," which indicate a group of "lives" according to the different sizes of companies. For example, one company may fall into the 100–249 lives size-band whereas another will fall into the 1,000+ lives size-band. While there is a great deal of consistency throughout the industry over size-bands, if one company decides to offer services for different size-bands or breaks down the existing size-bands at different points, meaningful comparisons in terms of how they are pricing their services become extremely elusive. For example, if everyone in the industry has a general category for 50 and fewer lives but one company decides to offer services priced for 25–49 lives, then gathering meaningful pricing intelligence in this segment of the market becomes more difficult.

Bids and Tenders

Then there is the competitive bid situation; although your company may be admirably qualified to provide a particular service or even be recognized as the industry leader, it is not a given that you will win the assignment if the project is put out to bid. This is particularly true with architectural and engineering services, with other building trades work, with ad and marketing agency work, meeting planning, and a range of other services. Competitive bids are frequently used in the public sector but are often also used by private companies. Here the challenge becomes not only finding ways to make your services, and thus the deliverables, stand out but also competing against the tendency of many traditional competitors to try to low-ball their bids.

What is obvious in such situations is that good pricing intelligence cannot be gathered "on the fly" while the heat of the bid situation exists. If yours is a company that is frequently asked to submit proposals or bids in competitive situations, and if you know the customer or client will not be single-sourcing, then intelligence work needs to begin well ahead of any particular bid and also be an ongoing activity to assemble the best pricing intelligence database possible.

The maxim "early and often" worked for an aerospace firm that regularly captured 80 percent of the dollar value of contracts available. At this firm, the modus operandi was to set up a formal capture team as soon as there was a hint that a contract might be in the offing. Several individuals at this firm were drafted to this cross-functional team and set to work to develop a winning strategy. The success of the firm rested on recognizing that the greatest opportunity to influence the buyers was in the early period, so initial efforts were directed to establishing rapport with decision-makers and influencers at each potential customer. Contacts with these people were frequent and used to gather information. Other sources of intelligence available in the public domain were also identified and tapped. The effort by the capture team was consistent and ongoing over the period of several years it often took before the bid was announced or the contract awarded.[1]

Just how close CI can get you to your target is illustrated in this case for a contract for diabetes supplies and services to be awarded by Novation, a large government purchasing organization (GPO) in the hospitals sector. The overall package being bid on included software and analysis tools as well as supplies to be used bedside with patients. To compete effectively and submit a winning bid, one of the larger healthcare services providers set out to gather intelligence about the competitor it seemed most likely to be compared to. With only a three-week timeframe to gather such intelligence, efforts were concentrated on speaking with buyers at hospitals where the competitor had accounts, other volume buyers (such as Premier), and contacts at the competitor itself. While the final figure the competitor planned to submit would have been an unrealistic goal, the investigating firm did get a range within fifty cents to a dollar of the price, meaning they were able to put in a very competitive bid.

Such competitive bid situations also raise the issue of what you are really competing against. As discussed in Part 1, it may be less the traditional competitors or the other providers of similar services and more the customers and influencers and their attitudes that form the competitive barrier. Understanding these organizations and the people who work there becomes essential to creating a basis for any pricing intelligence; in fact, the best pricing intelligence may have nothing to do with dollars and cents but rather an understanding of budgets at each organization, who controls them, what the agendas of these individuals are, and how the overall organization prioritizes its needs.

Is It Price or Cost
You Need to Know About?

Looking at this issue of how people price their services and how they compete on price raises an important related issue: costs. It is often difficult to understand a competitor's pricing, or compete against it, without first understanding the competing organization's cost structures: their overheads, labor costs, supply and equipment costs, client servicing costs, etc. Knowing their costs—or, at least, being able to make some fair deductions—enables you to understand how they arrive at their price.

To return to the examples of government competition, in the case of CORCAN (in Canada), the wages paid to the prison-based telemarketers are in the $1.50–2.50 CDN an hour range. In the for-profit sector, base wages for telemarketers are at least $6–7 CDN; in Canadian major metropolitan areas, minimums are often $9 CDN or higher an hour. Similar discrepancies between prison rates and minimum wages occur in the U.S., where the minimum runs between $3 and $5 per hour; the cost differential is not hard to spot here and quickly indicates how the government-backed service enjoys an advantage. Such cost advantages are not just the preserve of government-origin competition. Many times, your traditional competitors may enjoy more favorable costs and always be able to use this to gain an advantage. Looking beyond their prices to their costs makes extra sense when you face a situation where a competitor's pricing strategy seems suspicious.

Since many service businesses can be run on a shoestring budget, learning about their overheads can particularly be revealing. In Chapter 8, the need to learn where their offices are and how extensive the organization is was raised. This learning will dovetail nicely with studying costs. If a competitor has no office but is home-based, then its premises costs will be substantially lower than those of a firm maintaining an office. Serviced offices, which offer an address, phone service, and shared space, also cost substantially less; one advantage here, for an investigating party, is that the cost of such office space can be readily determined from the company running the serviced office.

If your competitor does maintain a fully serviced office of its own in commercial space, you can still learn about likely occupancy costs by identifying the broker who handles the building, or the property manager, and chatting them up to obtain both net and gross per square foot rates for the building in question.

Other facets of overheads include phone service, equipment, furnishings, and more. Reading the trade press and other business publications will keep you in the know. Companies often make announcements about their premises, especially if they have just undergone a facelift, and details along with the dollar costs do filter into the public domain.

The labor component of your competitors' businesses will be discussed in more detail in Chapter 15, but knowing how many people are full-time employees and how many of the staff are casual, contract, or freelance will give you the basis for extrapolating to get their labor costs. This is why it is also important to learn about marketing and the extent to which the public face of each competitor relies on smoke and mirrors; maintaining a mirage will always cost less than an organization of substance.

How Does It All Add Up?

Once you have a competing firm's costs and price, you have two of the building blocks to determining their overall sales and revenues. Even then, arriving at some figures for the size of the competitor's earnings will require more effort on your part.

The obvious first step is to see if there are any published data or formal revenue surveys you can tap. Here, it's important to remember these data will not necessarily be custom-tailored to meet your desires but will offer a starting point. For example, if you are in management consulting and your competitor publishes combined revenue totals for their accounting/audit practice plus their consulting arm, the published figure doesn't answer your question.

But it *will* give you a starting point to whittle away at. It helps focus your task and tells you what you are looking for, whether the combined revenues are $10 million or $10 billion. Now you know that the management consulting portion is *less than* this figure. It also offers you two avenues to pursue for coming up with the number you want; you can try to build a picture of consulting revenues or you can work by process of elimination, identifying and then *subtracting* the accounting/ audit portion of the business. Surprisingly, this latter tactic is often overlooked by people but, in many cases, elimination can be the easier strategy, no matter what services sector you're in.

One way to gain a sense of how a traditional competitor might be doing is to look at the intelligence you have gathered about their marketing initiatives and turn this inside out. The old adage about getting back out what you put in holds true for the marketing efforts and revenues of a service firm. For one thing, whatever marketing is going on has to be paid for; determining the level of direct mail, advertising, the number of "feet on the street" they have in terms of consultants going out to call on clients, all provide markers for which you can gauge the cost. This provides one half of the equation; the other is to gauge what kind of return they are getting in bids won or business landed.

There are other ways to start to learn about a competitor's revenues. For example, if you are in law, you can track your competitors' level of litigation: how many cases, how many years from start to finish for each case, likely number of hours billed, seniority of staff involved, and so on. Or, in the case of personal injury settlements or other contingency awards, you can track the size of these. None of this will produce an absolute figure overnight, but each provides a piece of the jigsaw puzzle and moves you closer to the answers you seek. You can always call up, or have someone do so for you, and learn the hourly rates of various lawyers, and use this as a starting point.

Similarly, in executive search, you can sort your competitors into fee-based firms and contingency firms. Tracking any ads such firms place will indicate the type of assignments they take on and the likely salary levels of the people they place. For contingency firms, you can deduce the placement fee from the salary; for fee-based firms, you can track elapsed time from ad placement to putting a candidate in the position and figure out how many hours were involved and the likely fee. It is time-consuming work but, if there are no published revenue data for your sector, such a method may be your only option. Similar strategies, utilizing both intelligence gathered and your own industry knowledge, can be used to deduce revenues in many services sectors.

Where to Look for Financial Intelligence

Some of the tactics for gathering intelligence about money have already been alluded to in the discussion above, but here is a recap of where you can look.

The obvious first step is to keep a lookout for any published price or fee data. This sometimes shows up in articles in the business press, when the award of a contract is announced and the dollar value of the contract is spelled out. Such intelligence needs to be captured at first sighting; it can be difficult to track down later. The types of ads known as "tombstone ads," placed after merger or other business deals have closed, also can indicate the dollar size of the deal and provide a point of leverage for further deductions about fees in certain sectors of the management consulting business.

Casual remarks dropped in conversation at professional meetings can also lead to snippets of price or fee intelligence. A service firm's literature or its Web site may even spell out for you what its prices are—or its revenue for that matter. Again, note the amount and the date you found it as soon as you do; if you go back later you may not be able to find the data, or an update to the Web site may have erased the figures.

Requests under freedom of information legislation, suggested in Chapter 11 to obtain copies of proposals, can work equally as well to gain fee/price intelligence, as what your competitors quoted for a particular piece of work will likely be given in the document. Such FOIA requests will tend to lead only to bids on government work, but this can be a valuable start. Or, if you operate in a jurisdiction where the public accounts are published, scan these for your competitors' names and the dollar value of any contracts they landed in the public sector.

What To Do With the CI You Gather

One of the first steps to take with fee/price intelligence is to see how your competitors' prices compare to your own. If you seem to be overpriced compared to other providers, you may need to either adjust your prices or take steps to emphasize the additional value-add you bring to the table. But, if you find you are undercharging, you may have the basis for raising your prices, provided your services offering is equivalent.

With cost intelligence, an analysis of how your costs compare and where your competitors' cost structures may give them an advantage is essential.

As for overall revenues, this will allow you to benchmark yourself against your true competitors, see how much business some of your imitators enjoy, and gauge the overall size of the pie and how much of it might be addressable by winning away market share from other players.

References

1. "Using Intelligence to Win Contracts." *Competitive Intelligence Review*. 1995: 12-19.

Tracking the Dollars

- Look regularly for ads for jobs, deals done, or other events that put money issues in the spotlight.

- Conduct regular searches for print and Web articles profiling traditional competitors: the more off-the-beaten track, the better. These will often reveal sales/revenue data.

- Visit trade shows or conferences where competitors have a presence and chat up their staff.

- Place FOIA requests for quotes or proposals filed with government, as these often yield pricing data.

- Scout out your competitors' locations or check Yellow Pages listings to see if the addresses used are shared or not, and otherwise determine the cost of their overheads.

CHAPTER 15

Who Are They?

Service firms rely heavily on their people to perform the services they offer and satisfy the customers; the argument could therefore be made that any service business *is* its people and nothing more. This means that a service firm, intent on understanding its competitors and its marketplace, needs to look into the personnel component of the firms against which it competes.

This can encompass a range of issues: just how many people there are, who the partners or owners are, which people are responsible for drumming up business, and more. Beyond mere numerical data, it's also essential to find out about the qualifications of a competitor's staff and what they bring to the table, as this has a direct connection to how the firm is perceived and how customers and influencers become competitive forces as a result. Just as sports teams are studied closely by their opponents to spot strengths and weaknesses, you need to undertake the same analysis of competing firms: Which ones are adept at going the extra mile? Which ones lack stamina in a crisis? Which have high integrity? Which are likely to muddy the reputation of the entire industry by way of sloppy work? As you go forward with your competitive intelligence gathering, learning about the people at your traditional competitors becomes essential learning.

How Many People?

While the number of people working at a competing firm might not tell you the whole story of what the firm can offer, obtaining a head-count does at least give you a starting point from which to proceed with further investigations. The number of partners or principals, associates or "partners-in-waiting," and support staff will reveal how strong a competing firm is. However, any services firm undertaking such an investigation needs to remain aware of how smoke and mirrors may be used to create the illusion of a firm that is larger than it is, as discussed in Chapter 8. Sophisticated telecommunications equipment now makes it possible, when you dial up any firm, to be faced with a lengthy menu indicating there are many people at a range of extensions. In some cases, this may be a perfectly true representation of the firm; in other cases, the voices could be those of long departed employees or temporary workers who are no longer with the firm. Sophisticated telecommunications equipment can also link together people who are not at a central office but are, in fact, based at home; such tactics cater to the customer's or client's need to feel the firms they are dealing with have what is known as "bench strength."

Another approach to studying the size and composition of competitors, which you may also find useful when piecing together a picture of each firm, is to remember the time-honored phrase "finders, minders, binders, and grinders." In a service firm of any size, there are people who go out and find the business, people who manage the business (minders), people who keep everyone working together and boost morale (binders), and people who actually do the work (grinders). How many of each there are will let you know where competing firms are strong or weak and how they are set up for the parts to work together.

Identifying the Owner

Another early building block in an intelligence gathering exercise is to find out who the owners of your traditional competitors are and what their objectives are for owning the firm. Here it's important to examine any assumptions you hold: Although you may *think* you know the ownership, your knowledge may not be up-to-date. Particularly with the smaller firms you compete against, they may have sold out to a larger entity or even one based overseas. Or, the original founder(s) may have sold the firm to an employee and might only be staying on board for a transition period. Such changes can herald a new strategic direction, a rebirth, or other initiatives, which awaken the "sleeping giant" potential in the firm, or introduce a lot of developments that will send you back to the drawing board to regather intelligence about the firm's services, marketing, delivery, and more.

Even if there are no major changes, knowing about owners will help you understand your competitors' strategies better and learn the direction they are moving in. Perhaps they own a services firm simply as a way to test the waters for new products they have in development—which may be common with IT consulting firms with links to software developers—or are they seriously committed to the core services of the firm and planning to build on these?

The ages of owners or partners are also important to learn because this can hint at the future fate of a traditional competitor. If the owners are in their 30s or 40s, then they may have no thoughts of retirement but will be looking to build up the firm as much as possible. Owners who are closer to retirement age may have other objectives, such as cashing in and letting another party run the business, all of which might suddenly change the competitive landscape for you.

Learning About Rainmakers

It can be important for an investigating company to know, from among the total number of staff, how many partners or principals work at a competing firm, because these are the people who likely go out and meet with clients and do the business development. In some industries, notably law, these individuals are known as rainmakers; the role of such individuals has already been raised in Chapter 11. If your firm has only one person in charge but your competing firms have two, three, or more, it is a fair deduction that they will be able to cover more territory to call on prospective accounts and drum up business than you will on your own, unless you have found methods to compensate for your lack of numbers, such as word-of-mouth marketing.[1]

Where Do They Come From?

Once you have the head count of a competing firm, you may wish to turn your attention to where they come from, their experience, and their qualifications. In certain sectors, such as accounting, law, insurance (actuaries), telecommunications, software consulting, and any health/medical service, the qualifications of the competing firm's staff and where such qualifications were obtained may tell you a great deal about the firm's strength and its prestige in the eyes of the customers. It is also a way to gauge how reliable any advice given by such firms might be and how thorough their educations are. In other words, is your firm competing against an organization with first-rate or second-rate staff?

This question was important to many existing real estate companies a few years ago when Century 21 burst on the scene. What had been a long-established industry, with very set ways, was shaken up by a company that took a different approach, particularly with its people, with compensation, training, and employee involvement in the business. Many firms suddenly wanted to know who these Century 21 people were, where they came from, and what made them tick.

It may also be prudent when investigating the backgrounds of staff members at a competitor's to determine where else they have worked in the industry. This can also tell you a lot about the work they might perform and their reputations. If, for example, your competitor mainly has staff who have never worked in the industry before, then this indicates that the firm might be at a disadvantage. However, if most of the people at a competing firm are industry veterans, this again indicates to you how strong your competitor's organization is.

Learning about the people at competing testing services was a core objective a few years ago when the Canadian Standards Association (CSA) wanted to expand its markets in the U.S. As mentioned in Chapter 4, government had changed the field of competition, under NAFTA, by removing the requirement that products sold in Canada had to be tested by CSA even if they had already been certified by a group like Underwriter's Lab.

CSA therefore began to look at the other certification firms around the U.S. This involved finding out where they were—some had one or two locations, others several—what they did and what staffing levels were.

In-depth interviews (one of the best ways to gather intelligence) were conducted with key contacts at each competing organization. This really unearthed the similarities and dissimilarities to CSA. Some organizations were very formal, hierarchical, and conservative, while others veered toward being mavericks, which led one CSA staffer to exclaim: "These people sound like cowboys!" But getting the flavor of each organization and learning more about its people gave a service business like CSA a much better tool with which to compete, as they knew what they were up against and could address any weaknesses spotted at competitors by building up CSA's strengths in their own marketing approaches.

How Long Have They Been With the Firm?

The stability of a competitor's staff may also be key information for you as you investigate. The willingness of the staff to remain on board provides continuity in client servicing. This means that when clients return with new assignments, the individual(s) who worked on the last assignment are still likely to be with the firm, which tends to contribute to the strength of the firm. On the other hand, if your competitors are experiencing high turnover of their staff, this may put them at a competitive disadvantage, especially if the customers or clients find out.

The example of the publisher that didn't take appropriate action over staff losses and suffered a lot of customer defections as a result was discussed in Chapter 6; knowing how long people have been with the firm also gives an indication of how well they may or may not be able to pull together. This may be essential learning if your competitors have both a sales organization and a service organization and the two do not cooperate. A few years ago, Canon wanted to learn about Xerox; the case illustrates the value of probing such issues. Although Canon sells a product, the key success factor in its business rests on the people it employs and how sales and service employees work together.

First, the locations of all the sales team as well as the service team had to be identified by using corporate publications, phone books, and electronic databases. Then, the proximity of sales offices to service centers had to be pinned down, which involved map study. This just gave the framework but did not reveal how the two interacted with one another.

This knowledge only came from calling up the offices and speaking with support staff, sales reps, service technicians, and field managers. (Had more time been available, a worthwhile extension of this would be to speak with customers and see if they felt the sales-service liaison was seamless.) Another wrinkle in the investigation was handling national or key accounts, which were dealt with separately by key account managers. This meant that there was another layer in personnel to learn about.

Exploring the interplay between these two arms of its competitor took time but proved valuable to Canon, which then used this as a template to restructure its own sales and service people to be more effective and ensure better staff retention.

What Do They Do, What Do They Know?

It is all very well to determine just how many people work at a competing firm and what their qualifications are: the real secret to understanding the competitive force they represent is to determine what they do. The service firm is really the sum of its parts; how the individuals who work there pool their intellectual capital is a significant part of what you compete against. The emphasis in many service businesses, especially the large management consulting firms, in recent years has been to provide solutions. Providing a solution to a client or customer means harnessing the skills of several individuals at the firm, from a variety of disciplines, and putting them to work on the customer's account. This was touched on in Chapter 10 in the discussion of integrated services. To fully understand this element of your competitors, you will need to look at the information you found about their head-counts, review the information you have about their qualifications and experience, and start to piece together how this all might coalesce to provide seamless service to the customers. This learning will form a natural partner to what you learned about their customer satisfaction levels from Chapter 13.

Knowledge is therefore the core expertise that service businesses offer, and how it is managed is key to each firm's success. In some firms, this will be an informal process: in others, formal knowledge management systems will exist. In studying your traditional competitors, you need to focus on two aspects of knowledge management

(KM): how the firm handles KM internally—and the aspects of this that are better than your own approach—and how this wealth of knowledge is communicated externally. (You should turn up CI about its communication of its knowledge to clients during your exploration of its marketing, delivery, and service as discussed in Chapters 11, 12, and 13.) If a competitor is better at KM, then you can use its ideas to improve your own processes.

An exploration of these issues starts with the cataloging of a firm's expertise, as already outlined, but then needs to focus on other issues, such as how the individual practitioners at the firm keep up to date. Some updating will stem from the assignments they handle; intelligence about these assignments can be garnered from any public domain announcements of business the firm has landed along with informal chats at industry events and networking meetings.

The other side of the coin, the formal or deliberate part of updating, can be learned by determining the continuing education such individuals undertake. Some education may be mandated by professional bodies, while other education may be voluntary and occur by enrollment in seminars and conferences offered by commercial seminar companies.[2]

Who Do They Know?

Dovetailing with this issue of what an individual consultant or the entire firm knows is that of who they know. While client relationships obviously figure in the equation, the consulting firm's broader network is equally of importance and interest. This network can include influencers, government contacts (including politicians), and people at associations and other industry groups. The extent of the relationships enjoyed by any single service firm can be likened to a spider's web, offering a range of vertical, horizontal, and oblique connections within each firm, between the firm and its customers, and among the firm, its suppliers, and other constituencies.

This was why a broadcasting company decided to build a database of industry executives. Rather than leave understanding of the intellectual strengths and weaknesses of competing companies to random recall by its own staff, it decided to systematize the process. Industry publications were scanned for notices of appointments and promotions; annual reports were obtained. Whenever anyone had won an award, this was entered into the database; the composition of the committee making the award—and therefore the existence of relationships between committee members—was noted. This effort paid off handsomely when regulatory challenges surfaced in the industry and when consolidation started to occur. The most influential and well-connected individuals could quickly be found in the database and efforts to utilize their influence channeled accordingly.

Recruitment and Retention

All of these issues with the people who work at competing firms do not add up to much if your competitors are not adept at recruiting new staff as needed. Other authors have identified this issue of recruitment as being of great importance in service firms and therefore of equal importance as a competitive factor.[3]

The critical nature of recruitment is illustrated by the example of Ernst & Young, one of the Big Five management consulting firms that set up its own search firm in-house, to focus on identifying the best talent and recruiting it. Faced with the hot economy of the late 1990s and the left-field competition of declining unemployment referenced in Chapter 7, Ernst & Young had to go one step further and learn more about the recruitment practices of its competitors and whether or not they were bedeviled by the same problems in hiring talent.

This investigation involved finding out whether or not competitors had in-house recruitment initiatives, who was in charge, how hiring was occurring (Campus recruitment? Displaced older worker job fairs? Overtures to sole practitioners? Internet recruitment?) and the use of compensation, both tangible and intangible, as a lure. To gather this intelligence, Ernst & Young tapped its internal resources, the knowledge and connections of its staff, as well as external sources originating with or describing its competitors.

How Are They Retained?

Hiring the staff isn't enough to keep a service firm healthy, so another facet of your competitive intelligence gathering should be to look at what keeps them around. Compensation is one issue, and some of this intelligence may be unearthed during probes you make about finances (Chapter 14). Benefits and perks also merit investigation as well, since these may be tools your competitors are using to sustain competitive advantage over you. Benefits of the healthcare and retirement variety may also come to light during investigations about costs, but perks—such as on-site masseuses, day care, flextime, work-at-home programs, a company gym, or espresso bar—may be more hidden aspects of employee retention tools that you need to explore.

Mass Defections

Another development that merits analysis is the mass defection of a department or core group within the overall team at a competing organization. Perhaps the entire graphic design department at an ad agency has quit? Or all the corporate tax specialists at a law firm have left to form a new firm? This presents two issues of competitive significance: the weakening of an existing traditional competitor and the possible emergence of a new player. It also creates a situation where customers and influencers may start to exert more competitive influence, if they view such change as detrimental to their interests.[4]

Where to Look for Intelligence About People

Making sure you have the best intelligence about people requires tapping the broadest range of sources. Many of these sources have already been referenced for other uses, such as marketing or delivery, but they are summarized here for convenience.

Articles in the business press, trade publications, and numerous other sources will offer two avenues to learning about the staff at competing firms: when individuals at such firms are quoted or profiled in articles written by third parties, such as journalists, or when employees of your competitors actually write the articles themselves. Both will offer valuable insight along with data of a more factual or statistical nature, such as qualifications, head counts, and responsibilities.

Another good source of people information is the appointment notice, when someone is promoted or hired into a competing firm. Trade magazines, newsletters, city newspapers' business sections, and other sources feature such notices, which are usually a form of paid advertising. Your competitors may also be obliging enough to make it easy for you by listing staff members, their names, qualifications, and duties on the firm's Web site, so make a point of checking these regularly.

A further source about personnel and expertise is the commercial seminar brochure, where staff from competing firms may be making presentations. If you are not already on the mailing or fax lists for the major commercial seminar organizers, such as the Institute for International Research or the Canadian Institute, take steps to add yourself or a member of your own staff. As additional insurance, double-check that you receive such mailings or electronic updates from any associations to which you belong or which cover key customer industries; this step will tell you about facets of competitors' marketing initiatives plus their personnel.

To broaden your understanding of competing firms' connections, examine membership lists for political parties, professional associations, lobby groups, alumni associations, bicameral chambers of commerce, and the society pages of the newspapers and magazines like *Town & Country*. (This last item will also lead you to knowledge about the event-marketing activities of your competitors.)

What To Do With the CI You Gather

The intelligence you gather about people, plus the other forms of intelligence you have, will allow you to create a good understanding of each competing firm. This information can be structured into an organization chart or some other grid to give you a bird's-eye view of the opposing team.

You will also be able to utilize this CI on a case-by-case basis with clients. If you are bidding against Competitors One, Two, and Three with Customer A, you will be able to look at exactly who will write the proposal, who will present to the client, who will do the work, and who will manage the effort. This knowledge will allow you to play up your own strengths and minimize your shortcomings in your own proposal and presentation to land more business.

Another use of such "people CI" is to scout the ranks of competing firms for talent you may be able to lure away to augment your own team. The histories of the people, as you uncover these, will also allow you to spot any bad apples at a competitor and decide how to contain any industry damage that may result.

References

1. "Promoting the Professions." *Business Quarterly*. Summer 1997: 64-70.
2. "Knowledge Management and Competition in the Consulting Industry." *California Management Review*. Winter 1999: 95-107.
3. *Beat the Competition*. Basil Blackwell. 1989.
4. "The Changing Professional Organization." *Restructuring the Professional Organization*. 1998: Chapter 1, p. 1.

Probing About People

- Scan for articles in print and online sources to discover authors who work for your competitors or individuals employed at competing firms that have been profiled in articles.

- Monitor for appointment notices, professional society awards, exam results (e.g., for CPAs), and other accolades.

- Check alumni association publications, local/community newspapers, and similar sources to gather data about the "leading lights" at your competitors.

- Place yourself on the mailing lists for a range of commercial and nonprofit seminar brochures to learn when speakers from your competitors are presenting.

- Track publications from charitable groups and the society pages to spot the up-and-comers at competing firms.

PART 3

THE COMPETITIVE GAME

CHAPTER 16

Staying Ahead

By the time you reach this chapter, you will have already developed a better understanding of the competitive forces you face for your service business by reading the chapters in Part 1 and, from Part 2, a good idea of the various aspects of your traditional competitors you need to become aware of so you can tackle marketplace challenges and get the better of these competitive forces.

Now it's time to move beyond reading and thinking to prepare for taking some sort of action. Following is a discussion or blueprint for moving forward; additional ideas and sources will be found in the Further Resources section of this book.

Developing a CI Mindset

One of the first steps is to develop more of a competitive intelligence mindset at your firm and prepare to see the world through new eyes. This means taking a fresh look at all the information you encounter and seeing which subset offers the potential to let you understand both competition and competitors better in your day-to-day business life. Another change is to find ways to harness your staff if your company is more than a one-person operation; for CI to be really effective, everyone in the organization needs to have a CI mindset. To do this, you may need to ferret out seminars or other programs you can send key staff people to, or perhaps identify a consultant you can bring in to the company to impart the thinking skills and mental awareness necessary for effective CI.

As part of this process, you may equally want to become aware of any calls or contacts being made to your company where one of your competitors may be trying to tap into your organization to gather CI for themselves. Finding ways to defend your business against such incursions means making your staff aware this could be going on; undertaking what's usually known as counter-intelligence is also a necessary part of doing competitive intelligence.

What to Collect?

If your organization has never undertaken CI work before, you may not have a body of information to draw on to start analyzing your competitors and the broader competitive environment. What should you collect and where should you start collecting it? If everyone at the company has become aware of the need to do CI, you can first scrutinize all the places visited by staff who go out of the office and where they might be able to pick up literature or information originating with competitors. You can also take a look at the mail that comes in to your company; perhaps there are items currently perceived as junk mail that should instead be reviewed as sources of CI and otherwise kept?

Another question to ask is: What information aren't you receiving that you should be? If you compete against any organizations that are publicly traded, are you receiving their annual reports? Do you get their current press releases? Finding ways to place yourself on the mailing lists of any competing organizations as well as the lists for your major customers is another step to take. Further sources you need to consider include trade shows; any time there is a major exhibit in your city or in the nearest large center to you, you need to make a point of going to gather any relevant information about competitors plus customer and influencer groups.

These tactics are only a starting point but, once implemented, should start speeding the process of an information stream into your organization. The next question then becomes how to organize or systematize it. Although we live in the age of computers, the first step here is not to automate too soon. Just as how in the early days of automation it was considered important to have a good manual system before a company tried to automate a process, it's probably key that you first develop some sort of manual system and get used to working with the information while you determine what is the most useful and the least useful intelligence before you try to put it all into a piece of software. Even if your system is no more sophisticated than some paper trays, cardboard boxes, or plastic milk crates, labeled appropriately, such a collection and sorting depot will serve you well in the early days. You can have a box for each of your major competitors plus one for each major competitive force, such as customers and influencers. File pieces of information that arrive in the mail, along with any reports your people bring back, in the appropriate box and take the time, once a week, to review it. This may sound simplistic, but you will develop a much better feel for the sort of automated process you need if you first get a hands-on experience with the content side of the information.

Where to Start?

Once you start to gather some information and want to move on to analysis and utilization, you will next face the question of where to get started. The larger your organization is, the more complex this task, but there are some ways to cut it down to size. One is to take your largest customers, as determined either by the dollar value of the business they place with you, the volume of business, or some similar measure, and, using each in turn as a focal point, start to develop a sense of the competition these organizations represent—is it customer-driven? Is it mainly from influencers other than your primary contact elsewhere in the organization?—and the external competitive forces you reckon with for each of these customers, e.g., government, traditional competitors, etc. By building a profile of competition for each of these major customers, you will be much better placed to see patterns in the overall marketplace, as these will emerge from your analysis of the individual customer companies.

Another way to get started is to take key or major customers you've lost in recent years and would like to recapture and begin to do a customer-by-customer analysis for each of them, to determine the full picture of competitive factors that lost you the business so as to identify ways to win the business back. Again, by looking at all the facets of competition—internal at the customer, external in the marketplace—not only will you have a better understanding of competition at the micro-level for each of these lost accounts, you will probably begin to see some broader patterns reflecting the macro-level of competition.

A further way to rationalize the early CI process is to identify companies you'd like to win as accounts and study the competition you face for each. Again, this should be done on a customer-by-customer basis.

Only when you have undertaken some CI work on this micro-level, customer by customer, will you be equipped to move to extrapolation of the findings so you can make some assumptions about the broader marketplace. For example, if you face a certain set of competitive factors for all your lost accounts in a particular industry, you are on safer ground to assume that you face similar competitive factors for all customers in that industry. Trying to jump into the macro-level of the marketplace and do CI at this level right away will turn the task into one that is overwhelming and also one that would be unlikely to yield any intelligence you can leverage for new business.

Learn from the Past

While you are undertaking the customer-by-customer analysis, it is also a good time to go through your own internal information and see what additional insight you can add to the mix. If you frequently are asked to submit bids or proposals to land business with these customers, this is a good time to review past bids you lost to see who you were up against and who eventually won. This can help hone your understanding of your traditional competitors in specific industry sectors and what other factors, such as customer or influencer activity, doomed or helped you from inside the client organization. If you have not previously kept records of bids you have won or lost, now would be a good time to start keeping this information and adding it to your CI resources. Reviewing past proposals and bids won or lost will also help show you if your company is growing or not and, if not, which company among your traditional competitors is on the upswing. Spotting those which are growing can help you further identify those organizations you need to understand better, in order to leverage your CI for growth.

Collect, Read, Think, Analyze, Use

If you were hoping that CI would be a one-time activity that, once completed, would sit on a shelf or in a computer, ready for you to use as you see fit, this is not the case. Competitive intelligence work requires ongoing effort to be truly useful. This is why, from the very earliest days, when you maybe have no more than a collection of printed or hard copy materials, you will need to move frequently between collecting, reading what you find, thinking about it, analyzing what it means, and then thinking up ways to use it. For example, you may obtain a brochure from one of your traditional competitors that will tell you about their strategy and, in particular, their positioning. If you look at their positioning statement, you may be able to tie this to certain of their customers whom you have found reluctant to change to a new supplier (you). The competitor's positioning may also tell you why the influencers at the customer are so set against recommending any new suppliers. This may lead you to ruminate about who the staff are at your competitor and the expertise they bring to the table, which, in turn, shores up their positioning statement and intensifies their relationships with the customers. Since the whole thing is very circular, once you know how the pieces come together, you will be in a better position to figure out ways to break the circle and best your competitor in the marketplace. So from collecting, reading, thinking, and analyzing, you can move into using, such as with developing a better positioning statement for your own organization, hiring people to help back it up, and changing the way you approach the customers and tackle the marketplace.

Cost-Effective CI

For service firms of all sizes, finding cost-effective ways to tackle competitive intelligence is an important issue. And, as has been emphasized earlier in this chapter and throughout the book, one of the best ways to do this is to get the intelligence to come to you as much as possible. This means getting onto mailing lists and otherwise generating a flow of information into your company. When you cannot get the information to come to you, you need to find relatively inexpensive ways to get to it; an obvious way is to look at your competitors' Web sites, if they have them, but recognize that this is not a fail-safe method because many companies still do not have Web sites, and this situation will likely continue for some time. Alternatively, even when competitors do have them, such sites are not always kept up-to-date. They may also be repositories for anything from misinformation—wishful thinking by your competitors—through to disinformation where they deliberately post misleading information to lead competitive firms, such as yours, astray. You therefore need to look at ways that blend in with your regular activities, such as attending professional meetings or going to conferences and trade shows, or for opportunities where your staff who are out in the field anyway (salespeople, technicians, delivery people) can automatically pick up intelligence as they go about performing their duties.

Another way a service business, particularly a smaller one, can tackle this issue of CI cost effectively is to team up with college programs or business schools that are looking for placements or internships for their students. Frequently, such placements are worked by the students on a pro bono basis in exchange for experience relevant to their career goals. It is therefore possible to have a student come in for a period of several months and task them with updating and enhancing your existing system for CI. The advantage of this approach is that, over a period of years, you would get the perspectives of different people, which should enrich the whole process.

Making CI Pay

All the gathering, thinking, organizing, and the like will never deliver value if you don't consciously make the effort to use the competitive intelligence you gather. We touched on this earlier in this chapter, but just to reiterate, you need to continually be asking yourself: How can we profit from this information? There are many ways to do this. If your competitors have reduced their costs, you can study how their model can be used and adapted to your organization so you can reduce yours. If they have found new ways of delivering to the customers, what can be adapted to your situation? If internal strife has beset one of your traditional competitors, what is the likelihood that this will spill over and affect all players in the industry; how can you protect yourself? How can you take advantage of your competitor's weakness? These are just some of the questions owners of service businesses or their managers need to ask themselves, on a daily basis, to keep up-to-date and profiting from competitive intelligence.

CONCLUSION

An Eye on the Future

Given the increasingly important role of service businesses in the economy, it can be expected that their importance will soon influence government and other central agencies and change the way economic and other data is kept and tracked. Currently, census data tends to lump together all forms of services, including white collar professions and blue collar trades, while offering census data users finely detailed breakdowns of manufacturing activity, activity which now accounts for less than 20 percent of the GDP. As the 21st century unfolds, it is hoped that better central data will become available to anyone operating a service business or who wishes to study services.

A further change that can be expected is that there will be more analysis and study of the services sector at the academic level, something which is now lacking. Except for a few large services type concerns, such as financial services, airlines, software development, and management consulting, services is noticeably lacking from the lists of case studies and other documents produced by academia. For this situation to turn around, academics and similar researchers will need to get over their obsession with measurement because one of the facts about services is that there are many aspects that cannot be measured. For example, there is the whole element of goodwill; if a service firm has a receptionist who recognizes clients' voices and greets them by name before they introduce themselves, this has a huge impact on the customers, although it cannot be measured because the customer's experience of it is subjective in nature. Service business activity is riddled with these types of realities that do not lend themselves to measurement but are nevertheless an important component of services.

Once more attention is paid to the services sector by both government and academia; it can be expected that better information will be available about all aspects of running and managing a service business, not just the element of doing competitive intelligence in services. Once this occurs, there will be more published information, such as case histories of CI in services, which were lacking at the time this book was written.

Services sector businesses will not be able to rest on their laurels at this point, since the type of left-field competition referenced in Chapter 7, never mind all the other forms of competition referenced, will continue to bedevil the operator of any service firm. The developed countries have not yet even begun to come to terms with the impact the Baby Boomers' retirement will have on their economies, as well as the advantage that will accrue to other nations, such as Japan and Singapore, where there was no Baby Boom to begin with. The emergence of stronger economies overseas will change the economic and, therefore, competitive landscape quite severely in the first half of the 21st century. Competition will also be significantly changed as sleeping giants like China wake up or the former communist countries of Eastern Europe and Russia stabilize and move to stronger market economies. Similar competitive threats could arise from South America or even some African countries.

And when the dust settles on the current technological revolution, those in the services sector may be surprised to find both businesses and consumers thrust back to relying on services closer to home rather than utilizing foreign-based services overseas. One of the factors driving this trend will be that technology will neither offer the panacea some believe it will nor will it be nonexistent nor just too expensive to use; as labor costs rise overseas, the technology that links companies in the developed nations to what had been low-cost producer countries overseas will no longer offer an advantage. Another factor that may work against such a dominant role for technology will be environmental issues and demands placed on electric generating capacity; it is not inconceivable that some form of electricity rationing will occur, meaning that purchasing a service from halfway around the world will not seem nearly as attractive as driving up the street to obtain it locally.

Economic downturns or downsizings at very large organizations will also continue to represent a competitive threat in the services sector, as such contractions foster the rise of a host of small service businesses, which increases the amount of competition and splits the available business up between a greater number of suppliers. This could lead to lower per capita earnings for many individuals, which in turn reduces their incomes, causing them to ration their own purchases of goods and services. Such chain reactions characterized the economy in the 1990s, and such a downturn may well mar the outlook for service businesses, large and small, in the first decades of the 21st century.

On the plus side, change always creates opportunity and new needs, some not yet known, will arise over the next 5 to 10 years and offer entrepreneurs new business potential. One of the characteristics of service businesses, which can be set up more quickly than a goods-producing business, is that whole new industries can spring to life very quickly.

Issues with health, the food supply, education, and caring for the elderly represent just some of the arenas where new businesses will be formed. Environmental restoration and alternate sources of power generation represent two more. How does this all relate to competition? What will be the competitive forces such new services businesses will face?

It is not possible to predict exactly what these will be, but it is possible to say, with some certainty, that competition will continue to emerge both internally and externally and that savvy service business managers, whether entrepreneur-owners or hired guns, will protect themselves by keeping an open mind about competitive forces and making no assumptions about who is or isn't a competitor. Instead, they will use a book like this as a blueprint for gathering intelligence, using it to hone their understanding of the competitive landscape and turning highly competitive situations to their advantage, so their businesses will truly be smart services.

Bibliography

"Bank of Montreal: Investore." Ivey Management Services. 1999: 23.

"Beyond Products: Services-Based Strategy." *Harvard Business Review*. March-April 1990: 58-67.

"Call Centre In Prison Has Union Crying Foul." *Globe & Mail*. March 2, 2001: A1, A6.

"Call-Net Enterprises Inc. Challenges and Opportunities In a Continually Changing Environment." Ivey Management Services. 1998: 17.

"Change in an Autonomous Professional Organization." *Journal of Management Studies*. July 1991:375-393.

"The Changing Professional Organization" in *Restructuring the Professional Organization*. 1998: Chapter 1, p. 1.

"The Charles Schwab Corporation in 1996." Stanford Graduate School of Business. August 1997: 15 + exhibits.

"CI in a Newly Competitive Marketplace: A Case Study of the Electric Utility Industry." 13th Annual SCIP Conference Proceedings. March 25-28, 1998: 149-158.

"Competitive Intelligence in Health Care Delivery." 15th Annual SCIP Conference Proceedings, Poster Session. March 29-April 1, 2000: 227.

"Developing a World-Class CI Program in Telecoms." *Competitive Intelligence Review*. Fourth Quarter 1999: 30-40.

"E*Trade Securities, Inc." Stanford Graduate School of Business. July 1996: 15.

"Five Strategies To Make a Professional Services Firm Stand Out." *Globe & Mail*. November 6, 2000: M1.

"Global client's demands driving change in global business advisory firms." Chapter 3 in *Restructuring the Professional Organization*. 1998.

"Globalization and Nationalism in a Multinational Accounting Firm: The Case of Opening New Markets in Eastern Europe." *Accounting, Organizations & Society*. 1998: Vol 23, #5/6.

Gordon, Ian. *Beat the Competition*. Basil Blackwell. 1989: 267.

"Jobs: How Long Can Services Pick Up The Slack?" *Business Week*. February 19, 2001: 34-35.

"Knowledge Management and Competition in the Consulting Industry." *California Management Review*. Winter 1999: 95-107.

"Knowledge Management at Ernst & Young." Stanford Graduate School of Business. September 1997: 19 + exhibits.

"The Launch of mBanx." Ivey Management Services. 1998: 22.

"Leadership Online: Barnes & Noble vs. Amazon.com." Harvard Business School. 1998, 2000: 21.

"A Link Between CI & Performance." *Competitive Intelligence Review*. Summer 1995: 16, 18, 20.

"Linking Competitive Intelligence to Corporate Strategy." *Competitive Intelligence Review*. Fall 1991: 21-22.

"Making Competition in Health Care Work." *Harvard Business Review*. July-August 1994: 131-141.

"Making Competitive Intelligence 'Sense' of the Financial Services Industry." 13th Annual SCIP Conference Proceedings. March 25-28, 1998: 251.

"Managing Assets and Skills: The Key To a Sustainable Competitive Advantage." *California Management Review*. Winter 1989: 91-106.

"Managing Knowledge and Relationships: Sustaining Success in Professional Services." Darden School Working Paper. 1996: 26.

Marketing Professional Services [seminar brochure]. The Canadian Institute. January 2001.

"Merging Professional Service Firms." *Organization Science*. May 1994: 239-257.

"Merrill Lynch & Co., Inc." Darden School Foundation. 2000: 17.

"Multi-tenant Retrofit Saves Time, Money." *Security Magazine*. August 2000: 24.

My California State Portal: www.ca.gov/state/portal/myca

"Note on the Consumer On-Line Services Industry in 1996." Stanford Graduate School of Business. July 1997: 21.

"Open Season: The CRTC Clears the Way for War in the Phone Business." *Maclean's*. May 12, 1997.

"P^2-Form Strategic Management: Corporate Practices in Professional Partnerships." *Academy of Management Journal*. Vol 33 #4, 1990: 725-755.

Peters, Thomas J. and Waterman, Robert H. Jr. *In Search of Excellence*. Harper & Row, 1982: 360.

Porter, Michael E. *Competitive Strategy*. Free Press, 1980: 396.

"Prison Industry Poses Unfair Competition." *My Business*. September-October 2000: 23.

"Promoting the Professions." *Business Quarterly*. Summer 1997: 64-70.

Rhode Island State Publications Clearinghouse: www.info.state.ri.us/azlist.htm

"Strategic Alliances within a Big-Six Accounting Firm." *International Studies of Management & Organization*. Vol 26 #2, 1996: 59-79.

"Substitutes: Your Next Marketing Headache." *Competitive Intelligence Magazine*. April-June 1998: 44-46.

UNICOR online: www.unicor.gov/schedule/index.ltm

"Using Intelligence to Win Contracts." *Competitive Intelligence Review*. 1995: 12-19.

"WFNX-101.7 FM and Boston's Radio Wars." Babson College, 1999: 28.

"What You Can Learn From Your Competitors' Mission Statements." *Competitive Intelligence Review*. Winter 1995: 35-40.

"Will Services Follow Manufacturing Into Decline?" *Harvard Business Review*, November-December 1986: 95-103.

The World Fact Book. CIA, 2000.

"Wrongful Dismissal, Corporate Foul Play, Medical Negligence." *R.O.B. Magazine*. January 2001: 36-40, 42, 44.

"You And Your Job" (questionnaire) Buffalo and Erie Jobs Coalition.

Further Resources

The number of books, periodicals, Web sites, and other tools available to support CI efforts in a service business is limited. Most publications and resources are geared to the goods-producing sector. However, here is a list of basic sources and other items that can be used as a starting point. Service business owners and managers are encouraged to explore beyond what's presented here, to identify sources they can tailor to their own company's unique situation.

Techniques

Here are some publications that will walk you through the intelligence process or provide "how-to" information.

Competitive Intelligence Magazine. Society of Competitive Intelligence Professionals, bimonthly.

Competitive Intelligence Review. Society of Competitive Intelligence Professionals, quarterly.

Fuld, Leonard M. *Competitor Intelligence*. John Wiley & Sons, 1985, 479 pp.

Fuld, Leonard M. *Monitoring the Competition*. John Wiley & Sons, 1988, 204 pp.

Fuld, Leonard M. *The New Competitor Intelligence*. John Wiley & Sons, 1995, 482 pp.

Halliman, Charles. *Business Intelligence Using Smart Techniques*. Information Uncover, 2001, 212 pp. Discusses text mining and the use of secondary source materials.

Miller, Jerry P. et al. *Millennium Intelligence*. CyberAge Books, 2000, 276 p. Includes a chapter on small business intelligence.

Sawyer, D. C., ed. *Tradecraft: A Compendium of Competitive Intelligence Techniques*. Information Plus, 1999, 86 pp.

Sawyer, D. C., ed. *Tradecraft: A Sourcebook of Competitive Intelligence Tactics*. Information Plus, 1995, 63 pp.

Vine, David. *Internet Business Intelligence: How to Build a Big Company System on a Small Company Budget*. CyberAge Books, 2000, 438 pp.

Business Information Sources

Here are some books and other sources you can tap to identify time-honored business information sources, which are the "staples" for business researchers in a range of industries. Their coverage of service businesses will vary.

Daniells, Lorna. *Business Information Sources*. University of California, 1993, 725 pp. Long considered the "Bible" of business information sources.

Directory of Business Information Resources. Grey House Publishing, annual, 1662 pp. Accuracy may vary, but services sectors covered include: Accounting, Architecture, Broadcasting, Business Services, Engineering, Finance, Legal Services, and Real Estate.

Encyclopedia of Business Information Sources. Gale, 2000, 1,200 pp.

How To Find Information About Companies. Washington Researchers, 2000, 606 pp.

KM World: Creating & Managing the Knowledge-Based Enterprise. Information Today, Inc. 10 issues per year.

Lavin, Michael R. *Business Information: How To Find It, How To Use It*. Oryx Press, 1992, 2nd ed.

Researching Service Companies & Industries 2000. Washington Researchers, 2000, 232 pp.

Statistics

Berinstein, Paula. *Finding Statistics Online*. Information Today, 1998, 356 p. Coverage is broader than business and examples tend to focus on goods-producing industries but text is still useful.

U.S. Bureau of Census. *Census of Service Industries*. Decennial. Based on Census data, gathered during designated Census years.

Government Filings

The Sourcebook to Public Record Information. 2nd ed., BRB Publications, 2001. Gives addresses and other starting points for tracking down material that traditional competitors have filed with government, and for placing requests under the FOIA legislation.

Case Histories

Case histories available from business schools are often a good source of discussions about service businesses, although the focus on competition and competitive issues will vary from case to case.

Babson College, Ph: 800/545-7685
(c/o Harvard Business School Publishing)

Darden School, University of Virginia, dardencases@virginia.edu

European Case Clearinghouse, in the U.K., Ph: 44 (0) 1234 750903 or e-mail ECCH@cranfield.ac.uk, in the U.S., Ph: 781/239-5884 or e-mail ECCHBabson@aol.com; www.ecch.cranfield.ac.uk

Harvard Business School Publishing
800/545-7685 or e-mail: custserv@hbsp.harvard.edu
www.hbsp.harvard.edu

Richard Ivey School of Business, University of Western Ontario,
519/661-3208 or e-mail: cases@ivey.uwo.ca
www.ivey.uwo.ca/cases

Stanford University, Graduate School of Business, Ph: 415/723-2835

Associations

Sources listed below are either specific to service firms or will lead
you to groups useful for networking.

Canadian Society for Marketing Professional Services, Vancouver, B.C.
www.csmps.com/

Centre for Professional Service Firm Management,
University of Alberta.
Ph: 780/492-3054

Directory of Associations in Canada, Micromedia, annual.
www.circ.micromedia.on.ca

Encyclopedia of Associations, Gale Publishing, annual.
www.gale.com
A good starting point to track down groups covering both cus-
tomers/clients and competitors. Headquarters can provide details
about local chapters and meetings in a business owner's area.

Society for Marketing Professional Services, Alexandria, VA.
Ph: 800/292-SMPS or 703/549-6117
www.smps.org

Society of Competitive Intelligence Professionals, Alexandria, VA.
Ph: 703/739-0696; www.scip.org
Contact the central office or check the Web site for chapter
meetings in your area.

Yellow Pages.

The phone book for your area should have a listing under "Associations" or "Societies" to lead you to local groups that customers or competitors may belong to.

Courses

The Competitive Intelligence Center, Simmons College.
Ph: 617/521-2809 or www.cic.simmons.edu

Gilad-Herring Academy of Competitive Intelligence.
Ph: 703/642-0884.

Fuld, Leonard. *The Fuld War Room™ - The Ultimate in Competitive Intelligence Training*. Harvard Business School Publishing.
Ph: 800/988-0886.

Society of Competitive Intelligence Professionals.
Holds programs plus local chapter meetings throughout the year.

About the Author

Deborah C. Sawyer is President of the Information Plus group of companies, firms providing research and consulting services to Fortune 500 corporations. Ms. Sawyer's client base, however, belies her in-depth understanding of smaller businesses in general and service businesses in particular: Ms. Sawyer has owned or continues to operate research companies, a business writing seminar firm, and a health consultancy. This gives her the inside track on what it's like to compete in services and how difficult it can be to learn about competition.

Prior to starting her first business in 1979, Ms. Sawyer was editor of two reference works for the education field. She holds two degrees from the University of Toronto and diplomas from the Canadian School of Natural Nutrition and the British Institute of Homeopathy. She is fluent in English and French, has slowly rusting ability in German, Russian, and Mandarin, and has travelled the world. When she isn't working, she paints in oils, sews, gardens, swims, walks, and reads voraciously.

She is the author of three other books about information and has published numerous articles. She also speaks frequently at conferences and has appeared on national television and radio programs in the U.S. and Canada.

Index

More Great Business Books from Information Today, Inc.

Millennium Intelligence
Understanding and Conducting Competitive Intelligence in the Digital Age

By Jerry P. Miller and the Business Intelligence Braintrust

With contributions from 12 of the world's leading business intelligence practitioners, here is a tremendously informative and practical look at the CI process, how it is changing, and how it can be managed effectively in the Digital Age. Loaded with case studies, tips, and techniques.

2000/276 pp/softbound/ISBN 0-910965-28-5 $29.95

Internet Business Intelligence
How to Build a Big Company System on a Small Company Budget

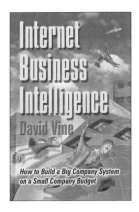

By David Vine

According to author David Vine, business success in the competitive, global marketplace of the 21st century will depend on a firm's ability to use information effectively—and the most successful firms will be those that harness the Internet to create and maintain a powerful information edge. In *Internet Business Intelligence*, Vine explains how any company can build a complete, low-cost, Internet-based business intelligence system that really works. If you're fed up with Internet hype and wondering "Where's the beef?," you'll appreciate this savvy, no-nonsense approach to using the Internet to solve everyday business problems and stay one step ahead of the competition.

2000/448 pp/softbound/ISBN 0-910965-35-8 $29.95

Internet Prophets
Enlightened E-Business
Strategies for Every Budget

By Mary Diffley

Since the bursting of the dot.com balloon, companies are approaching e-business with a new wariness—and rightly so, according to author and entrepreneur Mary Diffley. In *Internet Prophets*, Diffley speaks directly to the skeptics, serving up straightforward advice that will help even the most technophobic executive do more business on the Web. This readable, easy-to-use handbook is the first to detail the costs of proven e-commerce strategies, matching successful techniques with budgetary considerations for companies of all types and sizes. Unlike other books, *Internet Prophets* gets down to the nitty-gritty that every businessperson wants to know: "What's it going to cost?" Supported by a dynamic Web site.

2001/366 pp/softbound/ISBN 0-910965-55-2 $29.95

International Business
Information on the Web
Searcher Magazine's Guide to Sites and Strategies for Global Business Research

By Sheri R. Lanza
Edited by Barbara Quint

Here is the first ready-reference for effective worldwide business research, written by experienced international business researcher Sheri R. Lanza and edited by *Searcher* magazine's Barbara Quint. This book helps readers identify overseas buyers, find foreign suppliers, investigate potential partners and competitors, uncover international market research and industry analysis, and much more.

2001/380 pp/softbound
ISBN 0-910965-46-3 $29.95

The Invisible Web
Uncovering Information Sources
Search Engines Can't See

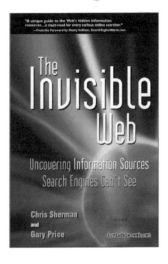

By Chris Sherman and Gary Price
Foreword by Danny Sullivan

Most of the authoritative information accessible over the Internet is invisible to search engines like AltaVista, HotBot, and Google. This invaluable material resides on the "Invisible Web," which is largely comprised of content-rich databases from universities, libraries, associations, businesses, and government agencies around the world.

Authors Chris Sherman and Gary Price—two of the world's leading Invisible Web experts—are on a mission to save you time and aggravation and help you succeed in your information quest. They introduce you to top sites and sources and offer tips, techniques, and analysis that will let you pull needles out of haystacks every time. Supported by a dynamic Web page.

CyberAge Books/402 pp/Softbound/ISBN 0-910965-51-X $29.95

The Extreme Searcher's Guide to Web Search Engines
A Handbook for the Serious Searcher, 2nd Ed.

By Randolph Hock

Foreword by Reva Basch

In this completely revised and expanded version of his award-winning book, the "extreme searcher," Randolph (Ran) Hock, digs even deeper, covering all the most popular Web search tools, plus a half-dozen of the newest and most exciting search engines to come down the pike. This is a practical, user-friendly guide supported by a regularly updated Web site.

2001/250 pp/softbound
ISBN 0-910965-47-1 $24.95

The Modem Reference
The Complete Guide to PC Communications, 4th Edition

By Michael A. Banks

Now in its fourth edition, this popular handbook explains the concepts behind computer data, data encoding, and transmission, providing practical advice for PC users who want to get the most from their online operations. In his uniquely readable style, author and techno-guru Mike Banks (*The Internet Unplugged*) takes readers on a tour of PC data communications technology, explaining how modems, fax machines, computer networks, and the Internet work. He provides an in-depth look at how data is communicated between computers all around the world, demystifying the terminology, hardware, and software. *The Modem Reference* is a must-read for students, professional online users, and all computer users who want to maximize their PC fax and data communications capabilities.

2000/306 pp/softbound/ISBN 0-910965-36-6 $29.95

net.people
The Personalities and Passions Behind the Web Sites

By Eric C. Steinert and Thomas E. Bleier

With the explosive growth of the Internet, people everywhere are bringing their dreams and schemes to life as Web sites. In *net.people*, get up close and personal with the creators of 36 of the world's most intriguing online ventures. For the first time, these entrepreneurs and visionaries share their personal stories and hard-won secrets of Webmastering. You'll learn how each of them launched a home page, increased site traffic, geared up for e-commerce, found financing, dealt with failure and success, built new relationships—and discovered that a Web site had changed their lives forever.

2000/317 pp/softbound/ISBN 0-910965-37-4 $19.95

Information Management for the Intelligent Organization
Third Edition

By Chun Wei Choo

The intelligent organization is one that is skilled at marshaling its information resources and capabilities, transforming information into knowledge to sustain and enhance its performance in a restless environment. The objective of this updated and expanded book is to develop an understanding of how an organization may manage its information processes more effectively in order to achieve these goals. The third edition features new sections on information culture, information overload, and organizational learning; a new chapter on Knowledge Management (KM) and the role of information professionals; and numerous extended case studies of environmental scanning by organizations in Asia, Europe, and North America. This book is a must-read for senior managers and administrators, information managers, and anyone whose work in an organization involves acquiring, creating, organizing, or using knowledge.

2001/softbound/340 pp/ISBN 1-57387-125-7 $39.50

Internet Blue Pages
The Guide to Federal Government Web Sites, 2001-2002 Edition

Edited by Laurie Andriot

Internet Blue Pages (*IBP*) is the leading guide to federal government information on the Web. *IBP 2001-2002* includes over 1,800 annotated agency listings arranged in U.S. Government Manual style to help you find the information you need. Entries include agency name and URL, function or purpose of selected agencies, and links from agency home pages. With double the coverage of the previous edition, *IBP* now includes federal courts, military libraries, Department of Energy libraries, Federal Reserve banks, presidential libraries, national parks, and Social Security offices. A companion Web site features regularly updated agency links.

2000/464 pp/softbound/ISBN 0-910965-43-9 $34.95

Super Searchers Do Business
The Online Secrets of Top Business Researchers

By Mary Ellen Bates
Edited by Reva Basch

Super Searchers Do Business probes the minds of 11 leading researchers who use the Internet and online services to find critical business information. Through her in-depth interviews, Mary Ellen Bates—a business super searcher herself—gets the pros to reveal how they choose online sources, evaluate search results, and tackle the most challenging business research projects. Loaded with expert tips, techniques, and strategies, this is the first title in the exciting new "Super Searchers" series, edited by Reva Basch. If you do business research online, or plan to, let the Super Searchers be your guides. Supported by the Super Searchers Web page.

1999/206 pp/softbound/ISBN 0-910965-33-1 $24.95

Super Searchers Cover the World
The Online Secrets of International Business Researchers

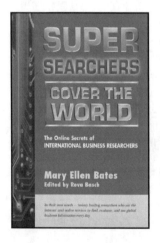

By Mary Ellen Bates
Edited by Reva Basch

The Internet has made it possible for more businesses to think internationally, and to take advantage of the expanding global economy. Through 15 interviews with leading online searchers, Mary Ellen Bates explores the challenges of reaching outside a researcher's geographic area to do effective international business research. Experts from around the world—librarians and researchers from government organizations, multinational companies, universities, and small businesses—discuss such issues as non-native language sources, cultural biases, and the reliability of information. Supported by the Super Searchers Web page.

2001/290 pp/softbound/ISBN 0-910965-54-4 $24.95

Super Searchers on Mergers & Acquisitions

The Online Research Secrets of Top Corporate Researchers and M&A Pros

By Jan Davis Tudor
Edited by Reva Basch

The sixth title in the "Super Searchers" series is a unique resource for business owners, brokers, appraisers, entrepreneurs, and investors who use the Internet and online services to research Mergers & Acquisitions (M&A) opportunities. Leading business valuation researcher Jan Davis Tudor interviews 13 top M&A researchers, who share their secrets for finding, evaluating, and delivering critical deal-making data on companies and industries. Supported by the Super Searchers Web page.

2001/208 pp/softbound
ISBN 0-910965-48-X $24.95

Super Searchers on Wall Street

Top Investment Professionals Share Their Online Research Secrets

By Amelia Kassel
Edited by Reva Basch

Through her probing interviews, Amelia Kassel reveals the online secrets of 10 leading financial industry research experts. You'll learn how information professionals find and analyze market and industry data, as well as how online information is used by brokerages, stock exchanges, investment banks, and individual investors to make critical investment decisions. The Wall Street Super Searchers direct you to important sites and sources, illuminate the trends that are revolutionizing financial research, and help you use online research as a powerful investment strategy. Supported by the Super Searchers Web page.

2000/256 pp/softbound/ISBN 0-910965-42-0 $24.95

Knowledge Management for the Information Professional

Edited by T. Kanti Srikantaiah and Michael Koenig

Written from the perspective of the information community, this book examines the business community's recent enthusiasm for Knowledge Management (KM). With contributions from 26 leading KM practitioners, academicians, and information professionals, editors Srikantaiah and Koenig bridge the gap between two distinct perspectives, equipping information professionals with the tools to make a broader and more effective contribution in developing KM systems and creating a Knowledge Management culture within their organizations.

Hardbound/ISBN 1-57387-079-X $44.50

Knowledge Management
The Bibliography

3 5282 00596 6448

Compiled by Paul Burden

Knowledge Management: The Bibliography is the first comprehensive reference to the literature available for the individual interested in KM, and it features citations to over 1500 published articles, 150+ Web sites, and more than 400 books. Organized by topic area (i.e., "KM and Intranets," "KM and Training," "KM and eCommerce"), this work is a natural companion volume to the ASIS monograph *Knowledge Management for the Information Professional* and an important new tool for anyone charged with contributing to or managing an organization's intellectual assets.

Softbound/ISBN 1-57387-101-X $22.50